Outrageous Justice

By

Craig DeRoche, Heather Rice-Minus, and Jesse Wiese

Outrageous Justice

ISBN: 978-0-9909222-4-7

Table of Contents

Foreword

By Christian Colson

During his days in the White House, my father, Charles Colson, had a front-row seat when President Richard Nixon launched the modern War on Drugs. It was the early 1970s, and during a public address, the president labeled drug abuse "public enemy number one." This national focus on the dangers of drugs and crime by our elected officials, and waves of subsequent "tough-on-crime" legislation, have contributed to America's current position as the world's leader in incarceration.

Shortly after leaving the White House, my father served federal prison time on a charge related to the Watergate scandal. He saw firsthand how even a comparatively short time behind bars affects people. He witnessed the despair, isolation, and lack of real opportunities for restoration. But he also began to see a purpose in his prison experience.

"I found myself increasingly drawn to the idea that God had put me in prison for a purpose," he recounted in his best-selling memoir *Born Again*. New to his Christian faith, he promised he would never forget the things he saw and the people he met there.

Not long after, in 1976, my father founded Prison Fellowship, now the nation's largest Christian nonprofit serving prisoners, former prisoners, and their families, and a leading voice for criminal justice reform. For more than four decades, this organization has helped restore those affected by crime and incarceration. Through Prison Fellowship and its many partners, God pours out His outrageous love and grace, replacing the cycle of crime with a cycle of renewal.

The hope of the Gospel is on the move in prisons across America, but much work remains. Behind concrete and razor wire, men, women, and youth are still warehoused—not restored. Families are still locked in generational patterns of crime. Our laws and culture still don't reflect the God-given dignity and potential of each person.

The problems plaguing our criminal justice system are many: over-incarceration, harsh and disproportional sentencing, a lack of rehabilitative programming behind bars, and untold obstacles that frustrate the efforts of returning citizens who want to contribute to their communities. As men and women revolve in and out of prisons, countless families and neighborhoods suffer on the outside.

In many ways, our complex justice system is rife with injustice from the moment of arrest to long after the moment of release. But we cannot let that paralyze us. Instead, it should motivate us to act.

God loves justice (Isaiah 61:8) and requires us to seek it (Micah 6:8). Can you imagine how much it must outrage Him to see the injustices in our system, which undermine the dignity and value of His creatures? Shouldn't it also outrage us and move us to change the situation?

This is not someone else's problem. The Church—God's plan for advancing His agenda on earth—has a scriptural mandate to visit the prisoner. But our mission must extend beyond evangelism and discipleship, as my father recognized in the 1980s when he started Prison Fellowship's work in criminal justice reform. Today, the Church still needs to make sure that the entire criminal justice system reflects God's passion for justice and becomes a place where lives can be genuinely transformed.

That's why the book you hold in your hands is so important. I know my dad would have been so proud of this resource, which explains in a compelling way exactly what needs to be fixed, what "justice that restores" looks like, and how ordinary Christians can work together to bring about necessary changes. This book is a manual for the next generation of Christian leaders who will visit prisoners, come alongside their families, care for victims, advocate for justice, and bring a long-awaited healing to America.

Yes, the challenges are many, but together we can bring about meaningful reforms. Consider this your personal invitation to join the movement my dad started more than 40 years ago—the movement for justice that restores.

Chapter One

Outrageous Justice

"*When I was 17 years old, I committed two armed robberies and went to prison for the next seven and a half years,*" Nick Robbins begins, telling the story he's told many times.

Nick shatters "ex-con" stereotypes. His boyish grin and brown hair are reminiscent of a young Tom Cruise. He looks like any young professional you'd meet at a concert or a sports bar, or in the cube next to yours at the office.

Every detail of prison life, Nick notes, "from the number they assigned me, 1155792, to the clothes you wear, it all reminds you of your greatest sin. What that did to my heart, was it hardened it. And what that did to my vision of my future, it became hopeless."

Nick grew up going to church twice a week, but most of his fellow prisoners probably wouldn't have guessed that.

Although prison is supposed to be harsh enough to keep you from ever committing another crime, Nick adds that life behind bars can sometimes have the opposite effect. In prison, he quickly decided he had to act tough to survive.

"Once you are thrown into that cage, you realize there are two types of people: the predators and the prey," he says. "And I had to decide, was I going to be the predator, or the prey? And I refused to be the prey. And that led me to enhancing my criminal activities."

When asked what that means, Nick flashes a grin again.

"I was a 17-year-old, 135-pound kid that looked like I was 12. I needed to make a name for myself. I needed to stand up for myself so that I wasn't going to get taken advantage of. So I found the biggest guy in the jail cell and started whaling on him. And after they released me from the emergency room and stapled my head back shut, I went back in there and continued that. The first prison I went to, I got kicked out of. The next prison I went to, I spent the first year in and out of solitary confinement."

Though foolhardy given his size, Nick's brazen aggression helped him gain the respect of other prisoners, who valued his toughness. But it also led to prison authorities extending his sentence. While behind bars, he continued to assault other prisoners in a misguided attempt to ensure his own safety and craft an identity. In other words, he was getting trained on how to be a more hardened criminal.

A criminal justice system that can turn a young man with a first-time offense into a violent criminal is seriously broken. Results like these are outrageous.

Nick's story (you'll hear more of it in a later chapter) is just a glimpse into a system which is plagued by injustice and produces a recidivism rate that may be as high as 79 percent.

We're naturally outraged by injustice. We're saddened and frustrated when we hear a story like Nick's, which confirms our fears that incarceration doesn't rehabilitate people, but often contributes to a culture of disregard for the law and the value of human life. While it may have been "just" to sentence Nick to prison for his crime, the prison environment seemed to be making things worse, not better. Was that justice? Was there a net benefit for society?

Land of the free?

America is called "the land of the free." Ironically, our country incarcerates more people than any other nation. About 2.2 million Americans are behind bars. Some need to be in prison, separated from society, because they pose a threat to the safety of others. About half of state prisoners, however, are incarcerated for committing nonviolent offenses like theft, fraud, and drug offenses. Others are unjustly convicted or sent to prison for violations that perhaps shouldn't even be crimes. Some end up in prison because they agree to a plea bargain, whereby they plead guilty to a crime they may not have committed, to avoid facing trial for a more serious crime and risking a longer sentence if they are found guilty.

As our society got "tough on crime" in recent decades, our criminal justice system grew exponentially. Harsher sentencing laws and charging policies, which call for lengthy prison terms that are often disproportional to the severity of the crime, caused the prison population to grow much faster than the general population. To make room for hundreds of thousands of additional prisoners, many new prisons were constructed toward the end of the 20th century, reflecting in concrete and barbed wire the rapid expansion of a criminal justice system that impacts the life of every American.

Disproportional sentencing isn't the only problem. Many new laws and regulations drafted in the recent past carry criminal penalties for offenses that might once have been addressed through civil or administrative means. There are now so many offenses carrying criminal consequences that no one has an accurate count of how many there are. Any American can break the law without knowing it.

Crime is a serious public issue, and our response, while serious, must also be *solution-oriented*. We must keep people who don't belong in prison from going there in the first place. Men and women behind bars, created in God's image, should be guided toward a crime-free, meaningful future that is available to them through the redemptive power of Christ.

Unfortunately, our criminal justice system often moves people like Nick in the other direction—hardening them, steeping them in criminal culture, and offering them no viable path toward making amends or rejoining the community. This is an outrage.

Act justly

When someone cuts us off in traffic, or takes credit for our ideas at work, something stirs in us. "That's not fair!" we think. We make decisions every day when dealing with kids, coworkers, and clients, in which we try to be "fair" but don't always hit the mark. We care about justice; we're outraged when it is thwarted.

"That's outrageous!" we might say, when we hear about someone who is punished too harshly, or someone, on the other hand, who gets away with little or no penalty for a crime. Why does injustice, even when it happens to other people, rub us the wrong way? We have an innate sense that wrongdoing should be punished, but fairly. We believe in proportionality—that consequences for wrongdoing should be neither too lenient, nor too harsh. Where does that finely tuned sense of fairness or justice come from? Why do we care about injustice?

We're created in the image of God who is pleased by justice but outraged by injustice. He has placed that same sense of justice in each of us and invites us to let it guide our actions.

Just behavior is right behavior. When we do the right thing, we are acting justly. Scripture also tells us that just behavior is a basic requirement for a good life.

> He has shown you, O mortal, what is good.
> And what does the Lord require of you?
> To act justly and to love mercy
> and to walk humbly with your God.
> (Micah 6:8)

While we are God's image-bearers, we have all also fallen short of God's standard of righteousness through our sin. We know what's right or fair, but we have trouble following through. As much as we are outraged by injustice, we sometimes behave unjustly, and we must proceed with caution when we are tempted to judge others.

God knows all too well that we will come up short each day. We will sin. Even when we don't act on the dark thoughts in our hearts, we certainly allow them more than we should. Recognizing our tendency to sin, an attribute we share with every person behind bars, we should hold humility in our hearts when we seek to hold another person accountable for their sin or crime.

Jesus taught us this posture of humility clearly when He disarmed a crowd bent on punishing an adulterous woman with the simple words, "Let any one of you who is without sin be the first to throw a stone at her." (John 8:7)

So, while most of us naturally grow angry when we hear about another person's sin, we should guard against the temptation to see those who have violated a law as "them," and we, who may be free of a particular sin, as "us." We should be outraged by wrongdoing, but as we seek justice, we must also remember that the person responsible is still of infinite value to our Creator. When we treat others justly and compassionately, we are reflecting the image of God and affirming it in others.

God's justice is intertwined with mercy and grace. We see this throughout Scripture, particularly in Jesus, who came to offer us grace, but also to fulfill the demands of justice by taking the punishment for our sins.

Because God is both just and merciful, He is not merely interested in ferreting out sin and harshly punishing it. He is interested in our rehabilitation. He invites us into transformation—that is, to put off sin and put on righteousness. The promise of transformation ought to give us hope that redemption is available to all of us, including every man and woman sitting in a prison cell today, no matter what they have done. And the personal transformation we have experienced as Christians ought to influence our concern for justice, since it is of great concern to God. As Paul, who spent a lot of time behind bars himself, wrote to the early Church:

"You were taught, with regard to your former way of life, to put off your old self, which is being corrupted by its deceitful desires; to be made new in the attitude of your minds; and to put on the new self, created to be like God in true righteousness and holiness." (Ephesians 4:22-24)

As we are transformed by Him, we learn to act justly, walk humbly, and love mercy.

A different approach

The American criminal justice system is in a dire state. It didn't deteriorate overnight, and it won't be repaired overnight. But there is hope, and there are concrete steps, based on enduring values and concrete evidence, that we can take collectively to fix it. The time has come for change.

But before we can take corrective action, it's important to understand the depth of the problem. Here are just a few key statistics:

- The United States incarcerates more people than any other country on the planet.

- One in 115 Americans is locked away in a prison or jail cell today.

- One in 38 people is under some form of government supervision through incarceration, probation, or parole.

- One in 9 African-American children attending our K-12 schools has an incarcerated parent.

- One in every 62 African-American men and one in every 93 Hispanic men are imprisoned, in comparison to 1 in every 365 white men.

At Prison Fellowship, we think these statistics are outrageous, so we advocate for change, for justice that restores. What do we mean by that?

As Christ-followers, we are not just to be concerned about justice; we're to *act* justly and to *advocate* for justice. We must respond to crime and incarceration in a way that is consistent with these priorities. This is not just our idea. It's a clear mandate in Scripture verses like this one:

"Speak up for those who cannot speak for themselves; ensure justice for those being crushed. Yes, speak up for the poor and helpless, and see that they get justice." (Prov. 31:8-9, NLT)

This book will give you in-depth insights about what's going on in our criminal justice system and how you can respond. It will give you the tools and inspiration to be able to obey God's command to not only feel compassion, but to act on your beliefs.

For more than four decades, Prison Fellowship, the largest Christian nonprofit serving prisoners, former prisoners, and their families, has been ministering to the incarcerated, who are among the most reviled and marginalized people in our society. The ministry was founded in 1976 by Charles "Chuck"

Colson, the "hatchet man" in President Richard Nixon's White House, who served seven months for a Watergate-related crime. Established on the belief that all people are created in God's image and that no life is beyond His reach, Prison Fellowship takes a restorative approach to all those affected by crime and incarceration. We strive to make prisons safer and more rehabilitative, advance criminal justice reforms, and support returning citizens, their families, and their communities.

Prison Fellowship staff and volunteers work inside prisons to share the Gospel and transform lives within the context of constructive, in-prison communities that foster lasting life change. We prepare men and women to be leaders in their communities—whether inside or outside of prison. As a result, we are seeing prisoners use their sentences as a time to grow, change, and find a new, positive life path through Christ. They're becoming part of the solution to crime by using their experiences to help transform others.

After 42 years, we have learned what works—and what doesn't. We have also come to realize that facilitating personal transformation in the lives of prisoners is just the beginning. We should visit the prisoner, but we are also called to pursue justice. When we become aware of unjust treatment and practices that fail to restore the lives of those in the justice system and the communities to which they return, we must seek systemic change.

Most American Christians do not visit people in prison and are uninvolved in pursuing justice reform. Why is that?

The answer is complicated. Our justice system is exactly that—a system. It can be hard to figure out how to approach it. We may assume that, because of bureaucracy, prisons will be as difficult for us to enter as they are for prisoners to leave. We may also feel that all prisoners are frightening, "other," or less deserving of our compassion than other people we might serve. But God's Word challenges us to work through those fears, challenges, and presuppositions to understand His heart for prisoners.

This book is about God's outrageous love for you and for every person—no matter who they are or what they've done. It's also an invitation to respond to that love by seeking justice that restores. Prison Fellowship has been working for justice reform for more than three decades. We've made a lot of progress, but we still have a long way to go. We believe that now, as violence, substance abuse, and a high incarceration rate plague our country, is the time for Christians to boldly step up.

The Church should engage thoughtfully in the national debate on criminal justice. We should demand a response to crime that holds people accountable while not discounting their innate worth. We need to think outside the bars, rather than treating incarceration as the default response to every crime. We should oppose disproportional sentences that degrade human value. We should validate victims and hear their voices. We should insist on policies, like protection from sexual assault, limits to the use of solitary confinement, and access to evidence-based rehabilitative programming, that create a constructive prison culture where people can be transformed. We should welcome back to our communities those who have served their time and are seeking to reintegrate as contributing members.

This book will unpack these issues and offer you clear steps to help you become an advocate for justice that restores.

Invitation to a journey

Perhaps you are already involved in prison ministry or have a loved one in prison. For you, the workings of the criminal justice system may be all too familiar. For others, the criminal justice system might seem confusing or intimidating. Perhaps you wouldn't even know how to begin to get involved or feel that your voice won't be heard. Our goal is to help you, no matter where you're at, determine your response to the biblical mandate to visit those in prison and pursue justice.

This book will help you understand what is going on in criminal justice these days and why it matters to every one of us. It will equip you to advocate for justice that restores, a concept Chuck Colson championed. "Criminal justice requires a just means to restore the domestic order as well as a punishment system that is redemptive," he explained in his book *Justice That Restores*.

To equip you to advocate in this capacity, we'll start by providing some basic information about just process in the next chapter so that you can understand and appreciate the strengths of our system—as imperfect as it may be. We'll outline what is legal and illegal, what we do to enforce laws, and what a person's rights are when accused of a crime. Just process and punishment are established by our government to accomplish clear purposes. We'll explore what those are and whether the system is advancing those goals.

We'll look at the history of the American justice system and the Church's involvement in it. We'll talk about victims, their rights, and what we can do to come alongside them. We'll wrestle with what proportional punishment means. We'll explore ways to advocate for more constructive prison environments that, while appropriately punishing wrongdoing, will help prisoners change and will make communities safer. We'll learn about the injustice of America's "second prison," where those who've served their time and paid their debt are still trapped, even though they are no longer behind bars.

Most importantly, this book will invite you to speak up on behalf of those who can't, bringing redemption and hope to the criminal justice system—and to our country.

Chapter Two

Justice That Respects:
What Is "Just Process" and Why Does It Matter?

*A*driana *had finally escaped an abusive boyfriend and was living in a women's shelter with her baby. She asked a friend at the shelter to watch her daughter while she ran to get some diapers from the store. A staff member at the shelter saw her leaving without her daughter after curfew, so she called the police. Upon returning with the diapers, Adriana was arrested and charged with endangering the welfare of a child.*

Before Adriana's arraignment, or first courtroom appearance, the public defender was unable to track down Adriana's friend. In court, nobody could confirm that her daughter hadn't been left unsupervised.

Although Adriana had no criminal history, the judge set her bond at $1,500 (the prosecutor had suggested $5,000). Adriana had no way to pay. Because of that, she spent weeks waiting in jail before her attorney was able to move the case to a different judge and finally get bail removed. By that time, Adriana had lost her bed at the shelter, and her daughter was placed in foster care.

Adriana's story is outrageous, isn't it? The system seems to have failed this homeless mother who was only trying to care for her child.

How did things get so off track? And how did situations like this one become so common? To understand what's going on, we have to take a look back at the formation of our laws and how our country's justice system has been set up.

When we talk about criminal justice, it can be easy to think only in terms of punishment for crime. However, justice involves a process that begins way before a punishment is handed down. It's based on a shared understanding of what is fair and just, and making sure people are treated according to those standards.

While how and why we punish those responsible for crime is incredibly important, we first must acknowledge how vital it is to have a fair process of determining guilt or innocence prior to sentencing. We've all seen television shows featuring this courtroom process, often depicting classic "gotcha" moments on the witness stand in a jury trial. However, courtroom drama shows don't accurately depict real life.

We have an opportunity and obligation to understand the real-life criminal justice system and its underlying assumptions. What does it mean for our process of punishment and conviction for crime to be just? And why is that so important?

God is just

Throughout Scripture, we see that God is deeply concerned with evenhandedness. God is a just God, and when sinful human beings could not measure up to His standard of holiness, He required punishment. We also know that God is the embodiment of mercy. Justice and mercy intersected at the cross. Justice was satisfied when Jesus, a sinless man and God's own Son, died, satisfying God's requirement for sin. Christ demonstrated mercy when He willingly took on our sin and accompanying punishment, allowing us to be exempt from God's righteous judgment.

God's desire for justice extends even farther than atonement for sin and provision of salvation. In fact, the Bible exhorts Christ-followers to live justly and love mercy in their daily lives.

For example, in the Old Testament book of Deuteronomy, God explicitly lays out rules for determining the guilt or innocence of an Israelite accused of a crime. These requirements include the specification that there must be at least two witnesses to prove guilt for a serious crime. Deceit by a witness was a grave offense.

You're likely familiar with the Scripture passage "an eye for an eye" (see Exodus 21:24). Despite how it's often misunderstood, an "eye for an eye" was not a prescription for revenge (which is often disproportional and emotionally driven) but rather, an instruction that justice should be limited, proportional, and fair—neither too harsh nor too lenient. The laws also served as a deterrent to crime.

Proverbs, the book of wisdom, frequently addresses the importance of fairness, identifying the need to administer justice in an impartial way and stand up for those who are most likely to be victimized in an unjust system, including the poor, foreigners, widows, and orphans (see, for example, Proverbs 31:9).

The New Testament carries forward this theme of impartial justice. The apostles spoke to the Church about treating people equally, without regard to appearance or wealth. They addressed the need for unity, oneness, and equality. Justice, including a just process, is part of God's perfect character, and a calling given to His people.

As followers of Christ, we should be motivated to uphold protections of just process in criminal procedure not only because we know that fairness is important to God, but also because we believe that each person has been created by God with inherent value.

Jesus summarized it simply. In Matthew 7, as a part of an extensive sermon on how to live, Jesus says that the Law and Prophets (in other words, most of the Old Testament) are summarized in one maxim: treat others as you wish to be treated. This principle applies not only to some people some of the time, but to all people all the time. As Christians, we are to respect and value every person as an image-bearer of God by treating him or her as we would like to be treated.

Although the criminal justice system is complex, our mandate is straightforward. To honor our Creator and follow His instruction, we are to advocate for the rights of others as though they were our own. Understanding the importance of justice, and its equal application to all people, is an imperative outpouring of obedience to a just Creator God. In contrast, the failure to adhere to and willingly pursue just process is morally and spiritually wrong.

God is outraged by injustice

Over and over in the pages of Scripture, we read about God's concern for the marginalized. While the law applies to all His people, God often makes special note of those who are likely to be taken advantage of: widows, orphans, aliens, and the poor. God is outraged by injustice, and He knew us well enough to know that the poor and powerless are more likely to suffer it. God sees the clear link between poverty and unjust treatment and warns us not to take advantage of those with fewer resources.

For example, God tells His people:

"Do not oppress a foreigner; you yourselves know how it feels to be foreigners, because you were foreigners in Egypt." (Exodus 23:9)

"Defend the weak and the fatherless;
uphold the cause of the poor and the oppressed.
Rescue the weak and the needy;
deliver them from the hand of the wicked." (Psalm 82:3-4)

"He defends the cause of the fatherless and the widow, and loves the foreigner residing among you, giving them food and clothing. And you are to love those who are foreigners, for you yourselves were foreigners in Egypt." (Deuteronomy 10:18-19)

"I know that the LORD secures justice for the poor
and upholds the cause of the needy." (Psalm 140:12)

Despite God's clear instructions, the poor have been oppressed throughout history. Without question, finances continue to be a barrier to justice. For example, Adriana, whose story you read at the beginning of this chapter, had to stay in jail because she did not have the money to post bond. Six out of 10 of the men and women in jail are simply awaiting trial, meaning they have not been convicted of any crime. Most jurisdictions rely on a money-based bond system, which means that rather than asking if the person accused of a crime is a flight risk or a danger to the community, the question that ultimately matters is, "Can they pay their bond?" If they can't, they will often remain in jail awaiting trial, sometimes for years! That's outrageous, and it flies in the face of God's concern for justice for the poor.

A majority of people in jail awaiting trial are there because they cannot afford to pay bond. Thus, people living in poverty are at a great disadvantage, not only in terms of the real-life impact of pre-trial detention like losing housing, jobs, or custody of children, but also in terms of the pressure to accept a plea bargain.

In some cases, a plea bargain allows a person accused of a crime the opportunity to be released from jail sooner than they would if they waited to go to trial. Because of this, even when someone is innocent, they will sometimes plead guilty just to avoid the long waiting period in jail.

A look back at the justice process through history

As we discussed in Chapter One, human beings have an innate sense of justice. A quick tour through history demonstrates our efforts to build fair and just societies and establish just processes by which to govern ourselves.

Not only are we familiar with Moses implementing a system of law and justice over Israel, but some of humanity's earliest secular manuscripts document concern for equitable application of law. As early as Hammurabi's rule of the Babylonian Empire (1792-50 B.C.), leaders issued an organized set of laws for their subjects to follow.

In the introduction to the Code of Hammurabi, the Babylonian king declared that his purpose was "to make justice visible in the land, to destroy the wicked person and the evil-doer, that the strong might not injure the weak." Though Hammurabi's code is not one that we would look to for guidance in setting proportional terms of punishment today, it displayed an early understanding of the need for a uniform system of justice.

Thousands of years later, Europe was grappling with a similar need for just process under a feudal system of government. Because the system gave privilege and power to a few by subjugating the masses, equitable rules of justice were nearly unheard of. In fact, during the reign of King John of England, the government charged outrageously high fines to citizens who wanted to obtain simple rights, such as a marriage certificate or the right to appear before the courts of justice. In response to these failures of King John, the Magna Carta was drafted in 1215. Drafted as a peace treaty of sorts between the king and several powerful barons, the Magna Carta promised the provision of certain basic rights and protected the people from illegal imprisonment while providing more reliable access to justice.

Five centuries later, Sir William Blackstone, an English judge and politician, published *Commentaries on the Laws of England*. These commentaries, written in 1765, heavily influenced the authors of America's founding documents. In his writings, Blackstone acknowledged three primary rights belonging to each person: personal security, personal liberty, and the right to private property.

Blackstone also identified the foundation of all law to be in the Creator. The impact of this understanding on America's governing documents can't be overstated. Reflecting Blackstone's view of the origin of law, the American Declaration of Independence boldly declares

> … all men are created equal, that they are endowed by their Creator with certain unalienable Rights, that among these are Life, Liberty and the pursuit of Happiness—That to secure these rights, Governments are instituted among Men, deriving their just powers from the consent of the governed …

This concept of unalienable rights is paramount in any discussion of preserving and championing just process in criminal law. Understanding that all human rights are derived from a just Creator God is the bedrock of any conclusion that humans have inherent dignity, and as such are equally entitled to justice regardless of their condition, color, or creed.

Christian influences on justice

Since the birth of the Church, Christians have played a significant role in advancing justice. The Bible influenced the development of justice in Europe and was central to the language and principles of America's founding documents.

That is not to say that those pursuing justice in the name of Christ have always or fully adhered to His teachings. Christians and non-Christians alike look back at history and rightfully critique misguided events like the Crusades or the Salem witch trials. The Declaration of Independence's recognition of the "unalienable rights" from our Creator was a critical step forward in building a fair justice system, but, of course, even this step was initially tainted by its acceptance of slavery and denial of rights to groups like women and minorities. Then and now, many of the gaps and faults in the criminal justice system result from failure to consult or even consider marginalized groups.

Despite our blind spots and failures, Christians have an overarching history of working for justice for all people, including prisoners. While we don't have the space to explore every aspect of the Church's involvement with criminal justice, it's important to note that the Church has long been a voice for justice and has advocated for fair treatment and rehabilitation of prisoners.

The early Christian Church granted asylum to people who had committed crimes and would have otherwise been mutilated or killed during the Constantine era. Prisons run by the Church became a substitute for capital punishment in medieval times, and correctional facilities developed by Christians in medieval Europe emphasized silence, prayer, and work. During the 18th century in America, isolation combined with intensive conversation with clergy became a popular practice, reflecting the belief that time for self-reflection would make prisoners penitent (hence the term "penitentiary"). (Unfortunately, the isolation contributed to prisoners' mental deterioration in some cases.) Another significant Christian influence on the penal system was the establishment of a regular chaplaincy, which provided education and counseling to men, women, and youth in prison.

Did Christians sometimes make mistakes as they attempted to rehabilitate wrongdoers? Yes. But they also sought to earnestly answer the call to visit prisoners and pursue justice.

While not all Christian experiments in the American criminal justice and penal systems proved effective or restorative, our history of engagement is something we hope Christians today will embrace. Grounded in biblical values and armed with an increasing knowledge about what works and what doesn't in the criminal justice system, we have a great opportunity to shape criminal justice reforms so that communities are safer, victims are respected, and lives are transformed.

Justice in the United States

While the Declaration of Independence recognizes the inherent dignity and value of all humans created by God, the United States Constitution expresses more direct protections of the rights endowed to each person. The Constitution is the pinnacle of American law and protects the rights of U.S. citizens through certain hallmarks of justice. Understanding these protections and their underlying ideals can help us recognize injustice in our system today. To understand how things have gotten off track, we first need to clearly understand how they were supposed to be. Let's review some basics about our government and laws, which will lay a foundation for our discussion in the rest of this book.

The Constitution reflects the founders' intense focus on protection of individual liberty. They wisely instituted a system of checks and balances that reflects a healthy suspicion of entrusting one group with overly broad powers. You could say that they recognized the sinful, self-seeking nature of man. As such, a large central government, composed of sinners, threatened the very liberties that the founders had fought so hard to attain. Without appropriate safeguards in place, liberty would have been forfeited. America's founding documents—the Declaration, Constitution, and Bill of Rights—set in place a system for achieving a just process in both criminal and civil matters.

There are several protections of just process available to Americans through the Constitution. These include: restrictions on search and seizure of property or persons, the right to remain silent in the face of questioning for criminal acts, the right to a jury trial for criminal charges, and the opportunity to be represented by defense counsel for criminal charges.

The Fourth Amendment to the U.S. Constitution offers protection of a person's property, as well as protecting people from unwarranted searches and seizures by the government.

Balancing the need for information to protect public safety (in part, by solving crimes) against the need for some level of personal privacy and ownership of belongings, the Fourth Amendment asserts that human dignity extends to exclusive ownership of personal property.

The Constitution also guarantees certain protections to those encountering a formal criminal charge. In the Fifth Amendment, the Constitution recognizes several rights related to criminal cases, including prohibiting trial twice for the same charge based on the same underlying facts and protecting individuals against making self-incriminating statements. The Fifth Amendment also requires that due process of law be provided before the government can take from a person their life, liberty, or property.

This right to "due process of law" includes guarantees that laws aren't unreasonable or arbitrary. It assures us that, prior to conviction, an accused person will have the chance to be heard at a time when proper notice has been provided—to have their "day in court," so to speak. The Fifth Amendment's protections work to provide a reliable, predictable system of justice that affords a person accused of a crime a full and fair opportunity to tell their own side of the story.

The Sixth Amendment notes several specific rights that protect a criminal defendant: a speedy and public trial, an impartial jury in the community where the crime was committed, information on the charges against the accused, the opportunity to cross-examine witnesses and to provide witnesses that are favorable, and assistance of an attorney for defense. Each of these rights activates at different times, and each protects a unique aspect of just process at a criminal trial.

These constitutional protections of just process are vital to a reliable system of criminal justice. If you personally are not involved with the criminal justice system, you may think these matters don't concern you. Remember that these protections are for everyone (although it took time and many legal battles to achieve the level of inclusion we have today, and they are not yet perfectly applied). Not only do they protect the rights of a person accused of a crime, they also provide guidelines for those who enforce our laws. They give a sense of predictability, peace of mind, and added security to all members of the community. Because these protections are critical to the well-being of our society, we must be strong advocates for their enforcement.

How can we "act justly"?

How do we act justly? We've established that human beings desire to create just societies and to offer just process to all. That desire for justice stirs within every human heart. Our sinful, selfish nature, however, would take advantage of power if we did not limit it. So how can we keep our own propensity to sin from undermining our desire for justice?

The same wariness of humanity's sinful nature that inspired America's founders to initiate our constitutional system of checks and balances on government authority, and to establish these protections of just process in criminal cases, should drive us to engage in robust advocacy on behalf of these protections. When we fail to limit the power of earthly authorities and pay attention to the rights of the least privileged among us, we can easily find that our culture and systems of justice have a weakened sense of fairness.

History offers many stories of injustice that resulted from people who were driven by fear or other factors to abandon just process and disregard the rules of a system instituted to protect the rights of both the guilty and the innocent. Jesus, for example, was not convicted under the due process standards of His time when He was put to death on the cross. There are plenty of modern-day examples, too, that show a failure to protect just process.

In 1987, a Georgia jury convicted a Black man, Timothy Foster, of killing an elderly white woman. The prosecutors in that case purposely removed African-American jurors from the jury, although they claimed that the jurors were removed for reasons other than their race. In 2015, the case finally reached the U.S. Supreme Court, and in May 2016, the court agreed with Foster that "the focus on race in the prosecution's file plainly demonstrates a concerted effort to keep Black prospective jurors off the jury."

Due process is also undermined if prosecutors knowingly conceal or withhold evidence that would help the defendant. This is blatantly wrong, but prosecutors rarely face any consequences for doing so. Although such practice has a name, a "Brady violation" (named for the *Brady v. Maryland* case, in which the Supreme Court decided prosecutors must turn over any evidence that would help the defendant), the law is written in such a way that it is hard to force prosecutors to comply.

Consider the case of John Thompson, an African-American man who was convicted of murder and carjacking, though he did not commit either crime. Prosecutors, it was later discovered, had not only ignored evidence, but willingly hidden it. Although Thompson was eventually set free, the prosecutors who put him in the Louisiana State Penitentiary for 18 years (including 14 on death row) were never disciplined.

Louisiana, and particularly the Orleans Parish, where Thompson was wrongfully convicted, has been faulted as a jurisdiction where prosecutors are given incredible power and held to very little accountability. No prosecutors were disciplined at all until 2005, and only two since then, "despite dozens of exonerations since the 1990s, a large share of which came in part or entirely due to prosecutorial misconduct." In other words, even though people were wrongly convicted, then exonerated of any crime, the prosecutors who put them behind bars in the first place faced no accountability.

As the power of prosecutors has grown, just process has eroded in many ways. While most prosecutors are in the profession to earnestly pursue justice, the lack of proper safeguards permits abuses. When so much power is available without proper limits or accountability, even well-meaning people can cross a line as they become consumed with "winning," or, in the case of prosecutors, obtaining a conviction. It's an area where Christians need to advocate for reform.

In the adversarial system of American justice, two parties, the prosecution and the defense, each present their case before a judge. In the criminal justice system, the government steps into the role of prosecutor, attempting to prove beyond a reasonable doubt that the crime was committed by the defendant. Though there are only two parties to a criminal case, there are more individuals interested in and impacted by the outcome.

Every crime impacts three primary interested parties: the person who allegedly committed the criminal act, the victim, and the community to which the harmed and accused parties both belong. A proportional administration of justice in a criminal case should result in appropriate punishment for the responsible party, validation for the victim, and a sense of justice and restored security for the community. The government is supposed to act as if it were the attorney representing the collective harms to the community and victim.

However, this system only functions effectively if certain rules of engagement, intended to protect the defendant's right to a fair and transparent process, are followed. These protections, preserved in our highest set of laws, apply equally to all. Norms that prohibit prosecutorial misconduct and protect just process ensure that a person charged with a crime has the opportunity for a speedy and fair trial, but they also protect civil servants, victims, and the community itself.

When just process isn't so just

Our responsibility to act justly includes speaking out against injustice—especially when injustice becomes systemic. We should be alarmed by three trends that have become commonplace: a growing use of plea-bargaining (which we mentioned at the beginning of this chapter), an over-burdened system, and an alarming number of wrongful convictions.

Prosecutors and public defenders are civil servants, paid by taxpayers to take part in the adversarial system of courtroom justice. Though most of these individuals are working hard at the difficult task of ensuring justice, the system is far from perfect. In fact, an increasing reliance on plea-bargaining has eroded the right to just process for many defendants.

In America today, less than 3 percent of those charged with a federal crime will see a jury trial. In fact, more than 90 percent of criminal cases are resolved through plea-bargaining, where a negotiation takes place between the prosecuting attorney and the defendant and his or her attorney, to agree to a conviction and penalty outside of court. As Professor John H. Blume explains, there are three primary reasons that these agreements are made:

> The first is the perceived need that all defendants must plead. The second is the current draconian sentencing regime for criminal offenses. And, the final contributing factor is that plea-bargaining is, for the most part, an unregulated industry.

With a code that criminalizes so many acts, and penalties that are frequently disproportional to the offense committed, the judicial system struggles with overwhelmed dockets. There are simply more cases than can possibly be heard through a trial. Plea-bargaining offers a way to resolve most criminal cases out of court, saving scarce time and money. A plea bargain allows a defendant to plead guilty to a lesser charge in exchange for the more serious charge being dropped. Defendants sometimes plead guilty to a lesser charge even if they are innocent of all the charges. Again, this is sometimes because if they insist on a trial to prove their innocence, they must await that trial in jail if they cannot afford bond.

At times, they are pressured into taking a plea deal because they are told they will probably lose in a trial, even if they are innocent. Not wanting to risk that, they take the deal.

It is perhaps even more alarming that, in numerous jurisdictions, defendants are allowed an Alford Plea. This operates like a standard plea bargain in that it allows the court to punish the accused; however, it is unique because it allows the accused to maintain his or her personal declaration of innocence.

The impact of this policy should startle us. With seeming eagerness, many people charged with crimes choose to plead guilty to a charge rather than risk the chance that they may be the recipients of a lengthy punishment—again, even if they know they are innocent. This heavy reliance on plea negotiation thwarts justice. It has kept many people from having a true opportunity to be heard.

Additionally, since 1964, our country has guaranteed the right to counsel for people charged with a felony who cannot afford an attorney. However, most public defender offices are overloaded with cases and employ insufficient numbers of support staff, limiting the capacity for quality defense to be provided to the poor.

As Christians, these issues should concern us. Government has credibility to hold people accountable only when it is also accountable to the public. To protect everyone's rights to just process, we must advocate for common-sense criminal code provisions, prosecutorial limits and accountability, and sufficient resources for public defenders for those who cannot afford their own attorney.

The potential for the erosion of just process is becoming glaringly obvious. Consider the rapid increase of known wrongful convictions. Since 1989, there have been more than 2,000 exonerations, and in 2017 alone, there were 139. These 2,000 individuals, who were falsely convicted, have wrongly served more than 19,000 years in prison!

Of the 139 exonerations granted in 2017, 51 were given to people previously convicted of homicide. Think about that: people accused and convicted of murder were cleared because a more thorough review of the evidence showed that they did not commit the crime in the first place! Of the 139 people released in 2017, 21 were sentenced to life without parole, 10 received life sentences, and 69 were cases in which no crime occurred. A majority of the false confessions noted in exoneration cases in 2017 were for homicide. Many were made by defendants under the age of 18 who suffered from mental illness, intellectual disability, or both.

According to the National Registration of Exonerations, 84 percent of those homicide cases also involved official misconduct by the police or prosecution. Seventeen of these exonerations took place because DNA testing revealed that the science used in the trial was erroneous, and 37 involved mistaken witness identification.

Imagine how these miscarriages of justice must break God's heart. These facts should stun and sadden us all and spur us to action. We have learned from Scripture that God, by His very character, is just. As Christians, we are to follow His biblical mandates to speak up on behalf of others and to help the needy.

We need a reliable system of justice that protects the rights of all involved, regardless of whether they are poor or rich, or proven to be guilty or innocent. We should advocate strongly for the protection of a system of just process and the increase of such protections, because our God loves justice, and we are each made in His image. Advocating for a just process protects the dignity and value of each man and woman He has created.

Chapter Three

Justice That Harms:
How Did We Get Off Track?

Lawrence Lewis worked as a janitor at a nursing home in the Washington, D.C., area. One day, the toilets at the nursing home began to back up. This unfortunate problem had happened before. Lawrence knew that the best way to deal with the problem, and the way the nursing home usually handled it, was to divert a sewer pipe, which he quickly did, protecting the nursing home residents from a potentially messy and hazardous situation.

The facility had diverted the sewer pipe to a storm drain outside numerous times before, because the staff believed that the storm drain led to the local water treatment plant. It was standard procedure, and it kept the nursing home residents from getting sick and the bathrooms from being contaminated. However, the pipe actually led to Rock Creek, which eventually ends in the Potomac River.

Lawrence, though he never intended to do anything wrong and was following standard procedure, was charged with violating the Clean Water Act, a federal offense. Although he had no criminal intent, that didn't matter. He pled guilty in a plea bargain to avoid going to prison. He had to pay $2,500 and was given probation, which included probation officers checking on him unannounced. His probation also required him to fill out monthly cash-flow statements showing his salary and his spending, to prove that he was not involved in anything illegal. Today, he has a criminal record, despite the fact he never intended to break the law.

One out of every 38 Americans is either incarcerated or under some form of community supervision, such as parole or probation. As a country, we have the largest incarcerated population of any nation on earth. It's outrageous, but how did we get here? Are there more people behind bars because crime has gotten worse?

To judge by the evening news, political rhetoric, or our social media feeds, society may seem to be increasingly violent, but the truth is that the violent crime rate dropped by more than 45 percent from 1995 to 2016. So if overall crime has greatly declined, why has the criminal justice system grown so much? Why are so many more people incarcerated today, for longer periods of time? Those are some of the questions we will explore in this book. If you think you're somehow immune to this epidemic, or not impacted by it, we hope this book will change your mind.

You might conclude, "Yes, we may have more people in prison, but we have less crime, so the system must have worked." However, to understand what's really going on, we need to dig deeper into the numbers. Researchers have broadly concluded that only a small fraction of the drop in the crime is due to increased incarceration, and the rest is attributable to a broad variety of factors like an aging population, more effective policing, and the economy. Many states have reduced their prison populations while simultaneously reducing crime. According to data from Pew's Public Safety Performance Project, the 10 states with the largest prison population reductions from 2008 to 2016 also reduced crime in their states by an average of more than 15 percent.

Focusing our attention on state or local statistics, which reflect greater uniformity in policies and enforcement compared to the overall national crime rate, can help us consider what is working to combat crime—and what isn't. In addition to understanding the causes behind the statistics, we need to ask what values our current criminal justice system is advancing. We want to challenge you to think beyond a utilitarian framework (one in which the end justifies the means) and start to look at our criminal system in a holistic and restorative way, applying a Gospel-centric framework.

Despite the clear flaws in our system, America has one of the better criminal justice systems in the world. As we said in the last chapter, we have a strong foundation for just process. While we certainly have some work to do, the rights of those accused of a crime in America are strong compared to most countries. However, our system's weaknesses must be addressed. As Christians, we need to ask some tough questions, because they impact every person in society, not just those who are in the system. What do we believe about crime, justice, mercy, and redemption, and where do those values belong in our criminal justice system?

Over the past several decades, a shift has occurred in how our society defines crime and justice and how we view those who find themselves, justly or unjustly, in the system. This shift is eroding the value of justice as well as the value of millions of men and women.

The criminal justice system: scope, terms, and players

Before we discuss the problems of our criminal justice system, it is important to start with some basic criminal justice terms. Other than lawyers and those who work in the criminal justice system, most people learn about the criminal justice system through popular culture. And while *Law and Order* may be entertaining, it is not the most accurate reflection of our criminal justice system or the people in it. So think of this chapter as a brief introductory course in criminal justice. To see how things have gotten off track, we first need to understand the basics of how the system is *supposed* to work.

The American federal government is made up of three branches (you may remember learning this in junior high). The executive branch, which includes the president, is charged with the enforcement of laws. The legislative branch, including Congress, composed of the House and Senate, has responsibility to create and change laws. The judicial branch, including federal courts and the Supreme Court, is charged with the interpretation of laws. Ideally, this structure allows for the power of government to be equally distributed among the three branches.

Additionally, each state has a three-branch government with similar responsibilities. There is also a third level of government that takes place at the local level. Local governments play a role in criminal justice through the passage and enforcement of local ordinances and the management of local jails.

Each of these levels—federal, state, and local—plays a significant role in operating the criminal justice system. Due in part to these overlapping responsibilities, the criminal justice system is an enormous bureaucracy, employing thousands of people and impacting millions each day. It also provides revenue for local, state, and federal governments from fines or sale of property seized through criminal or civil asset forfeiture.

Some of the most common players in the criminal justice system are: the defendant, victim, prosecutor, defense counsel, jury, and judge, defined below:

1. **Defendant:** a person accused of and officially charged with a crime. Defendants are presumed innocent until proven guilty beyond a reasonable doubt. A person should be charged with a crime only if there is probable cause that a crime occurred.

2. **Victim:** a person who suffered harm from the criminal actions of another person.

3. **Prosecutor:** an attorney employed by the government to prosecute a crime. It is a powerful position because prosecutors have discretion over such things as the level of criminal charges, plea agreements, and dismissals.

4. **Defense counsel:** a private attorney paid for by the defendant. If the defendant cannot afford a private attorney, a public defender will be appointed at the state's expense. This is called indigent defense and is protected by the Sixth Amendment.

5. **Jury:** a group of people who determine guilt or innocence in a criminal trial. The number of people on a jury can fluctuate depending on the level of the criminal charge.

6. **Judge:** a person, sometimes elected and sometimes appointed, who administers all criminal legal proceedings. Judges do not generally determine guilt but do have discretion over bail, admissible evidence, sentencing (unless expressly dictated by the legislature), and jury instructions.

Some of the most common terms used in the criminal justice system are arrest, bail, plea agreement, trial, felony, misdemeanor, mandatory minimum, jail, prison, probation, parole, reentry, and recidivism. Here's a quick rundown on these terms:

1. **Arrest:** the process where a person goes from being an ordinary citizen to a person accused of a crime, or a defendant. Upon arrest, a person is taken into police custody and formally charged with a crime.

2. **Bail:** collateral, generally cash, that is given to the court to secure a defendant's freedom from police custody. Bail acts as a pledge to appear at the next court date. This is also known as posting bond.

3. **Plea agreement:** an agreement of guilt between the prosecutor and the defendant, also known as a plea bargain. This is typically an agreement for less than the original criminal charges. More than 90 percent of all criminal cases are settled by a plea agreement.

4. **Trial:** the formal process for determining criminal guilt. A defendant may choose to have a jury trial, where guilt will be determined by a jury of his or her peers, or a bench trial, where guilt will be determined solely by a judge.

5. **Felony:** a crime that carries an incarceration period of over a year.

6. **Misdemeanor:** a crime that carries an incarceration period of up to a year.

7. **Mandatory minimum:** a criminal sentence where the minimum amount of prison time is mandated by the legislature, and the judge does not have discretion to deviate from that sentence. These sentences also require a minimum amount of time to be served before parole eligibility.

8. **Jail:** a holding place for people awaiting trial who have not been granted or cannot afford bail. Also a common

punishment for people sentenced to incarceration for a year or less. Jails are generally administered by local governments.

9. **Prison:** an institution that houses people sentenced to a year or longer of incarceration. Prisons are administered by state governments or by the Federal Bureau of Prisons. People convicted of a state crime with a sentence of a year or more will go to state prison, while people convicted of a federal crime with a sentence of a year or more will go to federal prison.

10. **Probation:** a criminal sentence that does not include incarceration but allows a person to remain in the community with some restrictions. These restrictions can include curfew, treatment requirements, or electronic monitoring. If a person breaks the conditions of probation, the original incarceration period can be applied.

11. **Parole:** a period of supervision that may follow a prison sentence. This is an early release from incarceration and may include limited movement and requirements such as employment, treatment, and drug testing. The federal prison system does not have parole. A person who violates the conditions of parole will be sent back to prison to complete the original sentence.

12. **Reentry:** the transition of individuals from incarceration to the community, which may involve using programs like job placement services, substance abuse counseling, and mentoring to promote effective reintegration.

13. **Recidivism:** refers to a person's relapse into criminal behavior or violation of community supervision rules, often after the person receives sanctions for a previous crime. Recidivism is evaluated differently depending on the jurisdiction but is usually measured by criminal acts that resulted in either re-arrest, reconviction, or return to prison during a three-year period following the prisoner's release.

The youth justice system has its own unique terminology. While this list is far from exhaustive, here are explanations of a few common terms:

1. **Adjudication:** similar to a conviction in the adult system, adjudication is the court process to determine if a youth has committed the act for which he or she is charged.

2. **Delinquent Act:** an act that would be prosecuted in criminal court if committed by an adult, but if committed by a youth, is prosecuted in juvenile court and carries different penalties.

3. **Status Offense:** an offense that is illegal for youth but not for adults, such as running away, underage drinking, and truancy.

4. **Truancy:** a violation of school attendance law.

Where are we?

Unfortunately, involvement in our criminal justice system has become part of the American experience, impacting an astonishing number of citizens. Most of us either have personal experience or know someone with personal experience. This impact is a result of the unprecedented growth of the criminal justice system over the past 40 years.

Let's take a quick accounting:

- More than 10 million arrests occur each year in the United States.

- One in 38 adults are incarcerated, on probation, or on parole.

- Approximately 2.2 million Americans are incarcerated.

- About 4.5 million people are on parole or probation.

- More than 2,000 people have been exonerated since 1989.

- Over 5 million children have a parent who has been incarcerated at some point during their childhood.

- Ninety-five percent of people who are incarcerated will be eligible to be released at some point.

- More than 600,000 people are released from jail or prison each year.

- Approximately 70 million Americans (one in three adults) have a criminal record.

- Black men between the age of 18 to 19 are almost 12 times more likely to become incarcerated than white men.

The cost of housing, feeding, and processing this number of people is staggering. States are spending approximately $70 billion on corrections every year. The Bureau of Prisons (the federal prison system) has an annual budget of approximately $7.1 billion and confines about 180,000 people, roughly half of whom are serving sentences for nonviolent drug convictions. This equates to our government spending about $39,000 per year to incarcerate each man or woman federal prison.

How on earth did the criminal justice system grow so big, so fast?

If you build it, they will come: the prison boom

The prison population in the United States hovered at or below 200,000 people from the 1920s through the early 1970s. After the 1970s, however, the prison population boomed. In fact, the number of people in prisons has grown exponentially over the last four decades. There were 667 percent more people incarcerated in 2008 than were incarcerated in 1972. As mentioned earlier, one in 38 Americans is under correctional supervision (incarcerated, on probation, or on parole). We have more incarcerated people than any other nation. Data shows that there are 1,719 state prisons, 102 federal prisons, and 942 juvenile correctional facilities. In 1950 there were just 158 prisons (combined state, federal, and juvenile).

To be clear, we need prisons. Some people present such a public safety concern that they need to be removed from society.

But unfortunately, incarceration has become synonymous with criminal punishment and has become the primary mechanism for carrying out justice.

We must never forget that criminal justice is about people first, people second, and people third. Incarceration affects individuals, families, and communities. Incarceration impacts not only the person but also his or her family, even for several generations. While a necessary tool, it should be considered only when the adverse impacts of incarceration do not outweigh the interests of justice. In other words, a person's punishment should not have more negative impact than the criminal act.

So, why the boom? Are people that much more criminal than they were in previous generations, or are other factors driving the growth?

Two of the primary drivers for the prison boom are the increase in sentence length and the increase in the number of criminal laws.

The War on Drugs and the expansion of mandatory minimum sentencing have played a large role in increasing the average prison term. People released from prison in 2009 served sentences that were on average 36 percent longer than people released in 1990. In other words, we are punishing people longer today for the same behavior they committed a generation ago. Unlike the dollar, the value of justice should not be subject to inflation.

Though the government has long sought to prevent drug abuse, the modern War on Drugs intensified when, as a response to the heroin epidemic seen in American soldiers returning from the Vietnam War, President Nixon declared drugs to be "public enemy number one" in 1971. In the 1970s and 1980s, as crime rates rose, police officials focused on street-level arrests, and judges, prosecutors, and corrections officials took a more punitive approach that emphasized the increased use of incarceration and lengthier sentences.

The War on Drugs was certainly a bipartisan effort, pursued by several administrations, both Democratic and Republican.

Only recently have we started to question these tactics from a values perspective. Are we restoring communities when we lock up people for lengthy periods as punishment for buying or selling drugs, but fail to address their underlying addictions?

Prison growth has also been fueled by the passage of mandatory minimum sentences linked to drug crimes. Eric Sterling, former counsel to the Judiciary Committee in the U.S. House of Representatives, talked to *Frontline* about the inception of mandatory minimums after Len Bias, an up-and-coming NBA basketball star, died of a crack-cocaine overdose. Here's what Sterling said:

> In 1986, the Democrats in Congress saw a political opportunity to outflank Republicans by "getting tough on drugs" after basketball star Len Bias died of a cocaine overdose. In the 1984 election, the Republicans had successfully accused Democrats of being soft on crime. The most important Democratic political leader, House Speaker "Tip" O'Neill, was from Boston, Massachusetts. The Boston Celtics had signed Bias. During the July 4 congressional recess, O'Neill's constituents were so consumed with anger and dismay about Bias' death that O'Neill realized how powerful an anti-drug campaign would be.
>
> O'Neill knew that for Democrats to take credit for an anti-drug program in November elections, the bill had to get out of both Houses of Congress by early October. That required action on the House floor by early September, which meant that committees had to finish their work before the August recess. Since the idea was born in early July, the law-writing committees had less than a month to develop the ideas, to write the bills to carry out those ideas, and to get comments from the relevant government agencies and the public at large.

One idea was considered for the first time by the House Judiciary Committee four days before the recess began. It had tremendous political appeal as "tough on drugs." This was the creation of mandatory minimum sentences in drug cases. It was a type of penalty that had been removed from federal law in 1970 after extensive and careful consideration. But in 1986, no hearings were held on this idea. No experts on the relevant issues, no judges, no one from the Bureau of Prisons, or from any other office in the government, provided advice on the idea before it was rushed through the committee and into law. Only a few comments were received on an informal basis. After bouncing back and forth between the Democratic-controlled House and the Republican-controlled Senate as each party jockeyed for political advantage, The Anti-Drug Abuse Act of 1986 finally passed both houses a few weeks before the November elections.

No hearings were held. No expert testimony was called. The legislation presented an advantageous political opportunity that would dramatically change our criminal justice system and millions of lives for decades, for better or worse.

In 1994, President Bill Clinton and Speaker Newt Gingrich came together to pass the Violent Crime Control and Law Enforcement Act. Otherwise known as "the crime bill," it required a state applying for federal funds for prison construction to demonstrate that it had increased the percentage of convictions of people with violent offenses and increased the average sentence imposed, often using mandatory minimums.

Mandatory minimums—applying primarily to drug offenses, murder, aggravated rape, firearm felonies, and repeat felony offenses—were the most frequently enacted sentencing change from 1975 to 1996. Getting tough on crime seemed like the sensible thing to do, and federal funds for prison construction provided a tempting incentive.

Unfortunately, this reactionary response to crime is more common in our history than one would like to admit. Much of the increase in our prison system can be attributed to reacting instead of responding thoughtfully to legitimate public policy issues. Drug abuse and crime are real public safety issues, but when we simply react, especially when motivated by politics, we create unintended consequences that have failed to solve drug addiction and lives lost to overdoses.

If you write it, they will come: the criminal law boom

Another reason for the prison boom is the expansion of the *number of laws* that can land a person in jail, or at least get them arrested, fined, and left with a criminal record. In fact, according to some estimates, the average American commits up to three felonies every day without intending to, simply because there is no way they know all the laws.

The responsibilities and duties associated with crime fighting have generally been understood to be an issue for state and local governments. Historically, this has meant that states have the police power to pass and enforce laws for the safety and general welfare of their citizens. This includes the ability to pass and enforce criminal laws. In fact, the first major federal bill that addressed criminal behavior was the Crimes Act of 1790, which only addressed about 20 crimes, many of which were related to treason and espionage. Today, however, there are more than 4,500 crimes specified in federal law, many of which duplicate state crimes. The federal laws are redundant. The structure of American government was developed to keep the response to crime local, but with the expansion of the federal government in the criminal justice arena, American citizens now need to be aware of federal, state, and local laws and regulations, all of which may carry criminal penalties.

Not only has the number of laws multiplied, but the definition of crime is also changing, making it easier for innocent actions, like Lawrence Lewis' diversion of the pipe at the nursing home, to be subject to criminal prosecution.

This practice, called over-criminalization, is an attack on the foundational principles of justice.

The ballooning of the federal criminal code

Determining the number of federal crimes in existence today is no small task. It has been estimated that Congress "enacted 452 new crimes over the eight-year period between 2000 and 2007—a rate of about 57 new crimes per year—for a total of 4,500 federal crimes in the U.S. Code." While this growth is alarming, it is only the tip of the iceberg. In addition to the nearly 4,500 statutory federal crimes, there are an estimated 100,000 to 300,000 federal regulations. You read that right: it has been estimated that more than 300,000 administrative code provisions may carry criminal penalties, but no one knows the true count. Average citizens cannot reasonably be expected to know the content of so many regulations, yet violations of any of these regulations may incur criminal culpability. The practice of over-criminalization overloads the already burgeoning criminal justice system, and the fact that Congress is directly exacerbating this problem by continually passing more criminal laws and regulations should concern us.

The over-criminalization trend has also rubbed off on states, including state juvenile justice systems. In 2015, the overall juvenile caseload was 1.6 times higher than it was in 1960. Zero-tolerance policies criminalize normal behaviors, like playground fights or skipping school, that were once handled in the principal's office, contributing to this troubling increase.

Why criminal intent matters

The Bible clearly says that the degree of a person's criminal culpability depends on their intention or mental state. Perhaps the best example of this in the Bible is where God delineated punishments for murder. According to Exodus 21:12-14:

Anyone who strikes a person with a fatal blow
is to be put to death. However, if it is not done
intentionally, but God lets it happen, they are
to flee to a place I will designate. But if anyone
schemes and kills someone deliberately, that
person is to be taken from my altar and put
to death.

Here, the Bible distinguishes punishment for murder depending
on whether the act was intentional. If the killing was intentional,
it was punishable by death, while a lack of intent was cause for
clemency. Additionally, unintended offenses were not punished
on the same scale as intentional offenses. (Read Leviticus 4-6 if
you're curious about Israel's first criminal code.)

The Bible emphasizes the importance of criminal intent in
dealing with guilty individuals. These values have continued
in our own culture for centuries. Indeed, criminal intent is the
line differentiating a crime from an innocent mistake. This
fundamental principle, however, is being eroded by Congress
in a misguided attempt to protect people and property. As a
result, Americans are in danger of a criminal justice system that
criminalizes commonplace, innocent behaviors.

Through the vast number of federal criminal laws and
regulations, and the lack of *criminal intent* requirements in
many of those laws, the federal government is criminalizing
activities undertaken with no reasonable intent to harm anyone.
For example, a person could face federal criminal charges and
time in federal prison for abandoning a snowmobile in a life-
threatening blizzard, digging up arrowheads, or even violating
another country's laws by packing frozen lobsters in plastic bags
instead of paper.

The pervasiveness and vagueness of federal laws and
regulations, many of which criminalize actions taken with no
criminal intent, should make us all uneasy.

How to fix over-criminalization

What can we do to address over-criminalization? With so many federal regulations already on the books, there are no easy answers. However, some proposed solutions are listed below.

1. Reevaluate criminal laws or regulations carrying criminal penalties. Remove those which do not merit criminal punishment.

2. Establish a default criminal intent standard. This remedy would allow courts to apply criminal intent in statutes and regulations where there is no criminal intent standard or where it is unclear.

Over-criminalization, especially in the "land of the free," is also a liberty issue. Every American should *know* if they are about to break the law and have the right to choose not to break it. Because there are so many laws—many capricious or vague— almost everyone is ignorant of the law on some level. When people are prosecuted for actions they never imagined could be crimes, it becomes challenging to appeal to conscience or virtue as guides to good behavior. Even when they think they are being "good," they might unknowingly be breaking a law.

The hidden cost

Beyond the financial cost to taxpayers, lengthy sentences, over-criminalization, and prison expansion have taken a toll on families. An estimated 2.7 million children in the United States have a parent currently behind bars. That's one in 28. In 1985, it was one in 125.

The problem is causing great harm, and to some groups more than others. Less than 2 percent of white children have a parent in prison, while about 11.4 percent of Black children do. That means a Black child is six times more likely than a white child to have an incarcerated parent. About 3.5 percent of Hispanic children have a parent behind bars.

Many of today's prisoners are children of prisoners, caught in a cycle of poverty, crime, and in some cases, injustice—which must be changed.

While we hear a lot about the number of Black men who are incarcerated, the number of Black women who are incarcerated is more than double the number of white women who are incarcerated. When mothers are incarcerated, they are separated from their children, who are often left with inadequate supervision, placed in foster care, or sent to relatives who did not anticipate and might not be fully prepared to care for them. The children are the ones who suffer, through no fault of their own.

What can we do?

Over-criminalization hurts all of us. The Bible tells us that we are to visit prisoners (Matthew 25:36). But when we consider the current state of criminal justice system and its impact on our culture, might it be even better if we tried to keep people from becoming prisoners in the first place?

Don't misunderstand. Crime should be punished, but the current system often exacts revenge instead of justice and treats incarceration as the default response. It hands out harsh sentences for nonviolent offenses, and children of incarcerated parents often pay the price.

Prison Fellowship believes that changes should be made to make our system fairer and more sensible. We advocate for justice that restores, and we hope that you will join us in trying to change the system so that victims and communities are protected, but people are not disproportionately punished.

In the chapters that follow, we're going to unpack some strategies for change. But before we do that, we need to begin by talking about the goals of the criminal justice system. That's where we'll turn our attention next.

Chapter Four

Justice That Restores:
Why Do We Punish Crime?

The day after a family vacation, Ismail Elmas went to work as he always did. When he didn't show up that evening, his wife, Jenn Carr, figured he was working extra hours to catch up after vacation.

When her husband still hadn't come home by bedtime, Jenn told herself he was still busy at work and went to sleep. When she awoke the next morning, Ismail still wasn't home. Beginning to panic, she called him and got no answer. She called a few of his friends. No one had seen him.

His friends went to his office, where they learned he had been fired the day before. Ismail, a financial advisor for more than 20 years, had mismanaged client funds and was in trouble.

Worried about her missing husband, she called the police. However, if Ismail wasn't considered a danger to himself or others, and had been missing for less than 24 hours, they could not file a missing person report.

Jenn began searching through emails and phone records, slowly uncovering a sickening truth: her husband had fled because he knew he'd committed a crime.

"In the end, there was a big hole that he had dug and couldn't get out of, and he was continuing to get deeper and deeper into trouble," she says. "He knew in his mind that this was not OK, that he was committing a crime, but he thought in his mind that he could fix it."

The phone records also revealed that he had gone to a former client's home after he'd left the office and had obtained a gun from that client. Because her husband was now armed, Jenn was able to file a missing person's report.

Eventually, her husband was found not far from their home. "He was scared and humiliated," she says. Because he had a gun and admitted to having planned to commit suicide, Ismail was taken to a psychiatric hospital for evaluation. Eventually, they let him come home.

"Our story just began to unravel from that point on," Jenn says.

As the truth came out, Ismail was charged with wire fraud. He'd mismanaged investors' money, but instead of admitting that, he dug himself deeper using other people's money. Those investors had no idea what was going on.

It became clear that Ismail was going to be incarcerated. What surprised Jenn was the sentence. He had to pay nearly $3 million in restitution and serve 10 years in federal prison. Convicted of a nonviolent, first-time offense, he had just been sentenced to missing a decade of his daughters' formative years.

"It was a shock to all of us, to my husband and me, to our children, who don't have their father at home anymore," Jenn says, her voice trembling. "They will graduate from high school without their father, they will go through life events without their father. Hopefully, they will not get married without their father walking them down the aisle."

At his sentencing, the courtroom was crowded with both victims and friends, some of them talking about how they'd been wronged, others asking the judge for leniency. In all, Ismail was convicted of defrauding 20 of his investment advisory clients of more than $3 million.

"The courtroom was full of victims," Jenn remembers. "Many of them were older people, whose stories varied, but all of them said that he was their friend and couldn't believe he had done this to them."

Ismail works a job in prison, and half of that income goes toward restitution. When he's released, he will have to continue to pay $500 per month toward it.

"My daughter wrote a letter to the judge, asking him not to give him a long sentence, so that he could be there for her, to support her." Jenn wipes away a tear. "I just don't believe the judge took that into consideration at all."

Jenn went back to work, taking on a full-time job and a second part-time job to provide for her family. She barely makes enough money to make ends meet and relies on others to help out.

"We have wonderful family and friends who support us and have helped us. God has provided for us in many ways, often in ways I don't understand. So we're grateful."

However, she notes, her husband is one year into his 10-year sentence, and the road ahead looks long and bleak. But Jenn is determined.

"My husband works every day to try to better himself, and to know that we still love him. And we're supporting him. Our family is intact, our marriage is still intact," she says. "I have chosen to take care of my family. We live on a day-to-day basis because that's all that we can commit to. I don't know what our future looks like at this point."

The family members and victims of people responsible for crime are often left wondering how their loved one could do such a thing. As happened in Jenn's case, they are also often left asking whether the punishment handed out is a just one.

Why do we use incarceration as a default form of punishment in cases where there isn't a clear link to public safety? Perhaps monetary restitution alone will not provide victims of financial crime with peace of mind, but will adding a term of incarceration make victims feel whole? Will it deter future criminal behavior or result in rehabilitation?

As we stated in the previous chapter, an outrageous number of people are tangled in the ever-growing criminal justice system. An estimated one in 38 adults is incarcerated, on probation, or on parole. Sometimes, this is due to policies, created with good intentions, that have gone awry. Being "tough on crime" sounds like an admirable goal, but it can result in unforeseen consequences, like unnecessary terms of incarceration that devastate families, that don't align with our goals.

In fact, there are times when what we call justice has become unjust.

Three traditional goals of the justice system

When someone commits a crime or harms someone else, something in us cries out for "justice." But what is justice? A starting point is "the righting of wrongs." But how do we ever right a wrong? We can't just wind back the clock.

Defining justice is difficult, but as believers in a God who loves justice, this is something we should wrestle with. One way to begin thinking about justice is to consider the purposes of punishment. Why do we punish people who commit crimes?

When we discuss justice, especially as it relates to crime and punishment, we can understand the actions of judges, juries, and policymakers as having one of three purposes: retribution, deterrence, or rehabilitation.

Prison Fellowship advocates for justice that restores, and we hope you'll join us after reading this book, if you haven't already. But first, we all need to understand the traditional goals of the justice system and their limitations. Let's briefly define each of these and then talk about how they align with our biblical values and a restorative approach to the criminal justice system.

Retribution is a term that has become associated with "revenge," but in its simplest form, retribution means to give what is due either as a reward or a punishment. It is an "eye-for-an-eye," or proportional, approach to criminal justice.

Retribution recognizes that every person is made in the image of God and therefore has value and potential. That doesn't suddenly change if he or she commits a crime. But, if they do something wrong, we need to respond. Their choices matter, and they need to experience the consequences of those choices. When our goal is retribution, we seek to punish wrongdoing in a way that is proportional to the crime committed and does not diminish that person's value as a human being. A proportional response also signifies the human value of the victim. In other words, if our justice system does not have a goal of retribution, we in effect say that the perpetrator is not worth the punishment and the victim is not worth the effort. Retribution says that a person must be punished for their crime, but not punished more than they deserve.

However, when we try to take a retributive approach, we run into the complex question of which punishment fits a crime. If someone has repeatedly committed a crime, but a juvenile commits the same offense for the first time, should they get the same punishment? Is that just? Mitigating factors can be part of what we weigh when we talk about retributive justice.

Deterrence is making an example of people who break the law to discourage others from that same activity, or to make that person think twice before committing another crime in the future. In a sense, all laws and their associated punishments are intended as deterrents. By informing the public about a law and the expected consequence if they break it, the leaders of a community presumably limit the number of people who will commit a given act. However, not all laws are effective deterrents.

Deterrence is based on a large (and often faulty) assumption: illegal behavior is a logical process. It assumes that before someone commits a crime, he will thoughtfully consider the consequences, saying to himself, "If I do X, then I will suffer Y."

In Prison Fellowship's decades of experience with the incarcerated, however, we have found that criminal activity is rarely an exercise in logical deduction. A member of a violent gang lives under the threat of injury or death but stays in the gang anyway. A person addicted to drugs could overdose but takes them anyway. When these very serious natural consequences fail to deter criminal activity, additional legal consequences may also fail to dissuade someone, because these decisions are not primarily rational.

In fact, when asked why they committed a crime, people often are at a loss to explain why, other than it seemed like a means to an end. They needed money, so they committed robbery. They were angry, so they assaulted their enemy. They were addicted, so they bought and sold drugs. Or, in the case of gang violence, they were sometimes simply following orders. They rarely weigh the consequences before acting. If people applied logic to crime, there would be a lot less of it.

For a criminal law to successfully deter crime, a lot hinges on implementation. Some shining examples of deterrence come from what has been called the "swift and certain sanctions" model. Such programs were developed to address common flaws in the implementation of community corrections, such as failure to connect repeated misbehavior to a consequence, or responding to a minor infraction with too drastic a consequence.

For example, a parole officer may not react when a parolee misses appointments or fails a drug test, because the law affords him no mild sanction. After allowing the parolee to continue the behavior without any deterrent, the parole officer, fed up with continued misbehavior, may then, on the seventh violation, send the parolee back to prison for years. The swift and certain model offers a different approach. It institutes close monitoring, swift and certain responses, and modest sanctions to better deter participants from misbehaving. It mandates a response much earlier in the process.

The HOPE program in Hawaii is among the most well-known programs utilizing swift and certain sanctions. It uses random and frequent drug testing for probationers who have used drugs and have had a hard time complying with the conditions of their probation in the past. By responding to every violation with a modest but consistent sanction (a few days in jail on a weekend immediately after the failed drug test, for example), Hawaii has achieved several positive outcomes, including lower no-shows for probation appointments and much lower rates of positive drug tests.

In South Dakota, the 24/7 Sobriety program has also used a similar model for people convicted of driving under the influence and has seen a 12 percent reduction in repeat arrests. The consistent and immediate sanctions involved in these programs are critical in terms of successful deterrence.

Rehabilitation comes in varying degrees and approaches, but this goal starts with the premise that people can change. Rather than just throwing someone in prison for their crime, we want to try to change them, hoping that will not only keep them from committing crimes in the future, but also will improve their quality of life. Sometimes, social ills like extreme poverty or untreated mental illness contribute to criminal behavior. Crime can be the symptom of other underlying problems. Rehabilitation focuses on trying to resolve those underlying issues as well as addressing common criminal thinking patterns.

For example, if a person is an alcoholic and gets arrested for drunken driving, we could just fine them or make them serve time in jail. But often, a person convicted of drunken driving will also be required to go to rehab or Alcoholics Anonymous meetings to address their underlying addiction. By connecting punishment to forms of accountability that are more effective at rehabilitating, the person may be able to get sober and stay that way, so they won't drive drunk in the future.

Of course, it can be difficult to measure rehabilitation. How much better do you have to behave to be considered rehabilitated? Justice is not necessarily satisfied when a person is "cured" of their bad behavior. We must always balance any rehabilitative efforts with the retributive or proportional punishment for the crime.

C.S. Lewis argued against rehabilitation as the primary goal of justice because, although it seems "mild and merciful," if it is the only method used, it denies someone their full human agency by saying that, as a product of their circumstances, they couldn't have made a better choice. He writes:

> To be "cured" against one's will and cured of states which we may not regard as disease is to be put on a level with those how have not yet reached the age of reason or those who never will; to be classed with infants, imbeciles, and domestic animals. But to be punished, however severely, because we have deserved it, because we "ought to have known better," is to be treated as a human person made in God's image.

Our criminal justice system does not advance retribution, deterrence, or rehabilitation exclusively. Historically, our system has sometimes swung more toward one goal or another, but it has always drawn from them all in some measure.

Our system of justice is rooted, in part, in the biblical tradition, so it's not surprising that we can find examples of retribution, deterrence, and rehabilitation in the Bible. None of these should be considered the perfect solution, but all of them are a foundation for justice that restores.

A restorative approach to justice

Our current system has a multi-goal approach, at least in theory. But as Christians, we need to think about what the best approach is. How do we advocate for justice that is biblical and restorative?

Justice that restores contains elements of rehabilitation, deterrence, and retribution. However, it goes farther because it looks at the big picture. It addresses the needs and rights of the victim and the community, acknowledging that crime impacts everyone.

Justice that restores doesn't just mean making someone do the time if they do the crime. It means holding men and women accountable to accept responsibility for the harm they have caused to their victims and communities, and to take steps to make amends and rebuild trust with their communities.

Healthy, spiritually fit individuals who have repented will seek to make amends either voluntarily or when an aggrieved party seeks restoration for an injustice. The types of amends and consideration that can right a wrong are as infinite as the forms of wrongdoing.

However, our government simply cannot demand voluntary exchanges of amends, repairs, and restorative efforts between the harmed parties and those who have done the damage. We can and should provide such restorative opportunities within our options for punishment, but our laws, rules, and sentencing guidelines must also provide other punitive consequences for those who do not avail themselves of those opportunities.

Prosecutors, judges, police, and policymakers are increasingly becoming aware that while incarceration is a necessary option, and provides powerful motivation for compliance, it is often less effective in restoring the victim and the community than an alternative sentence. Alternatives might allow for voluntary measures of contrition and direct amends to be offered by the person who has violated the law.

Incarceration takes away most of a person's freedoms and privileges. It is a serious punishment, but it is passive. For example, if someone breaks into a car to steal a laptop and is punished with a 30-day jail sentence, this does nothing to pay back the harm or loss to the victim or the community. In fact, it has significant costs to the community in taxpayer dollars. Incarceration requires compliance, but not a genuine effort by the convicted person to restore the harmed party. Therefore, our leaders are learning that having other forms of accountability, which offer more opportunity for active participation in restoring the victim and community, can better advance justice and reduce future crime.

If, instead of being sent to jail for 30 days, the person who stole the laptop must pay restitution to the victim, complete community service, and be monitored in the community, her or she is making amends directly to the harmed parties. The person is demonstrating initiative, and her efforts can lead to a more transformative outcome for the victim, the community, and the wrongdoer herself. Simply warehousing men and women in prison for years without any constructive opportunities cannot advance public safety, especially when 95 percent of people sent to prison are eventually released back into communities.

At Prison Fellowship, we believe there are many missed opportunities to infuse these restorative goals into the criminal justice system. Restorative justice programs, which focus on providing an opportunity for victims of crime to be heard by the person who harmed them and to develop an individualized restitution plan, can provide an alternative to incarceration or other traditional forms of punishment.

Chris Marshall, head of school at the School of Art History, Classics, and Religious Studies at Victoria University of Wellington, New Zealand, wrote:

> [Conservative American Christians] sense no tension between their support for a relentlessly punitive criminal justice system and the incessant call in Scripture to practice forgiveness and reconciliation, a call they conveniently confine to the sphere of interpersonal relationships within the Church. ... Knowing God's justice to be a restoring and renewing justice, the Church is obliged to practice restorative justice in its own ranks and to summon society to move in the same direction. There can be no justification for saying one thing about God's justice in Church and advocating the opposite in the world.

Marshall makes a fair point. We can't practice forgiveness and reconciliation in our personal relationships but advocate for harsh and disproportional punishment in the criminal justice system. It is our duty as Christians to advocate for our restorative values to be part of the criminal justice system. However, we must also acknowledge appropriate differences between our personal obligations and the government's duty. The state does not have the same obligation to "turn the other cheek," for example, that we are called to as believers. In fact, the state does not have standing to do so. Rather, the state has a duty to seek punishment that protects the public within the bounds of justice.

The state should dole out retributive sentences according to what is owed to the victim and consider utilitarian goals (that is, rehabilitation or deterrence) that serve the community, but as often as possible, the state can promote opportunities to facilitate relational or restorative justice.

For example, if a victim desires to opt for a restorative justice program or asks for mercy to be extended at sentencing, and doing so would not unduly jeopardize public safety, we would argue that the state should honor and facilitate such a request, and that this better serves the state's utilitarian goals.

Justice that restores should include rehabilitation, because it would be morally wrong to warehouse people for years in a prison cell and then let them out without providing the tools necessary for them to succeed. Justice that restores enforces the law in a way that deters crime, while advancing appropriate accountability and opportunities for rehabilitation.

As we think about punishment within a restorative framework, a fundamental question is whether a given punishment is proportional. That is, does it fit the crime? That is what we will explore in the next chapter.

Chapter Five

Justice That Fits: What Is Proportional Punishment?

At a low point in her life, fueled by addiction and the mistaken belief that the cash would help keep her family together, Debi, a mother of four daughters, and her then-husband began selling methamphetamine, or meth.

Selling drugs was, of course, not a great strategy for life improvement. It never is. Instead of keeping her family together, it tore them apart. Eventually Debi was arrested and charged with a federal offense. A woman to whom Debi had sold meth cooperated with prosecutors in exchange for receiving a shorter sentence. Debi was charged with conspiracy to sell 10 kilos (over 20 pounds) of meth based on the other woman's testimony, which Debi contested.

Debi had at first sold to only friends. Then she met someone who connected her with a person in Fort Worth, Texas, and Debi began shipping small amounts of meth there. While the quantity of drugs she'd personally sold was nowhere near 10 kilos, she had become part of a larger network of drug dealers. Conspiracy laws, designed to break up drug rings, allow federal prosecutors to charge everyone involved in the supply chain with the total quantity of drugs involved.

"I couldn't believe as a first-time, nonviolent offender, I'd be sentenced to 20 years in prison. There were no drugs confiscated, no evidence, just an informant trying to get out of a life sentence," she says. "It was just ridiculous."

Due to the federal mandatory sentencing guidelines in place at the time, Debi was sentenced to 20 years in prison. Her four daughters grew up in foster care.

After earning the maximum time credit possible for good behavior, Debi was released. Eventually, she was reunited with her now-grown children and grandchildren after serving 16 years.

Debi admits she deserved to be punished for breaking the law, and even believes that prison provided her a needed wake-up call. It was there that she got sober, obtained her college education, and was able to pursue a deeper relationship with Christ through a Prison Fellowship program. However, she believes harsh sentencing for people convicted of first-time, nonviolent offenses is not good for families or society.

As Christians, we often take heart in transformational stories like Debi's. Ideally, punishment serves a transformative purpose, as it did in Debi's case. We ought to be among those who remember prisoners, visiting them and valuing their salvation and God-given potential. We should celebrate redemption and growth that we see in any one of God's children, including those behind bars.

Nevertheless, when the type of punishment or length of sentence is disproportional to the crime, should our Christian duty to remember such men and women begin long before they enter the prison gates? Debi was sentenced to two decades for what she did. Did her sentence fit her crime? Or does it seem disproportional?

Proportional punishment

Justice, it's been said, is getting what we deserve. But how much is exactly what we deserve? What does justice look like when it comes to punishment? What is proportional punishment?

Justice in our country often misses the mark. Like Debi, instead of getting what we deserve, people sometimes get far worse punishments than seem to fit their crimes. Or to make matters worse, we punish in a way that leaves people more likely to commit another crime.

As Christians, we understand the need for punishment. Our God is a God of justice. From the very first sin, when Adam and Eve ate the forbidden fruit, God responded with punishment and consequences that continue to this day. However, God's response was tempered by mercy. Even as Adam and Eve were expelled from the garden, God gave them a promise of redemption and provided clothing, covering their nakedness and shame.

It's not a question of whether we punish wrongdoing, but how and to what end. The Scripture passage "an eye for an eye" (see Exodus 21:24) establishes that the punishment exacted should not be out of proportion to the crime committed. But does "proportional" mean that God literally requires an eye for an eye, a life for a life?

The proportionality principle is a foundational standard in many nations' criminal justice systems. In the United States, this standard is fleshed out in case law on the Eighth Amendment, which prohibits "cruel and unusual" punishments. However, criminal justice experts have a variety of opinions about what that phrase means.

The Supreme Court has gone so far as to establish a three-step test to determine proportionality. Step one: a determination must be made of whether the gravity of the offense and the severity of the sentence result in "gross disproportionality." Wait a minute. Does this strike you as a bit circular? To determine if something is proportional, we must first rule out that it doesn't strike us as incredibly disproportional. On what basis does one gauge what is grossly disproportional?

The second and third parts of the test are arguably more objective, requiring a comparison of similar offenses and associated sentences within a state and then across jurisdictions. This first part of the test, however, is considered a hurdle that usually must be fulfilled before moving on to the other parts of the test. As a result, we are back to a squishy gut notion of proportionality. Even if we get to steps two and three, the sentencing schemes in every state are always first rooted in what the legislature or judiciary believes to be proportional, or rather, "not grossly disproportional."

So, even for the Supreme Court, determining what proportional means is complex and much more an art than a science. The slogan "punishment that fits the crime" sounds simple, but we must each wrestle through determining what this means, and our judgments are colored by our understanding of the purpose of punishment.

So how should Christians approach this question?

We should start by grounding ourselves in the framework for justice that restores, which aims to provide a just punishment that will help restore all parties. As we discussed, a restorative approach seeks to address the harm caused to the victim and community, not only through a just punishment for the harm done, but also through opportunities for the responsible person to make amends, earn back the public's trust, and restore right relationships. Christians should advocate for restorative values to be infused into the criminal justice system, including when it comes to the type and length of sentences.

Advocating for justice

Given the far-reaching impact of incarceration in America today, and the powerful picture of justice that restores provided in Scripture, it's critical that we evaluate the various stages and issues associated with sentencing and punishment. We must consider where we can advocate for more meaningful opportunities for restoration of all those impacted by crime and incarceration and take action to advance fair sentencing.

First, as we discussed in Chapter Two, sometimes people are sentenced and imprisoned for crimes they did not commit. In 2017, 51 prisoners were exonerated for homicide crimes alone. That means evidence set them free. They collectively served hundreds of years in prison, and several faced the death penalty. It's essential for Christians to support the provision of defense for the poor and to advocate for a just trial process to protect the innocent.

And our duty also extends to the guilty. We cannot meet injustice with an injustice of our own. Excessive punishment violates human dignity just as much as turning a blind eye to injustice.

Let's consider the case of Weldon Angelos. Upon his first criminal conviction, he received a mandatory sentence of 55 years for selling a few pounds of marijuana over the course of three transactions. During the buys, he possessed a handgun, though he did not brandish or use it. The government prosecuted him under the federal statute 18 U.S.C. § 924(c), which required a five-year sentence for someone carrying a gun during a drug deal and a 25-year sentence for each subsequent offense. Although Congress intended to inflict the 25-year enhancement on those who had previously been caught, Weldon's offenses were stacked together for his first-time conviction.

Judge Paul Cassell, the sentencing judge, was thus required to give Weldon a mandatory 55-year sentence, despite being appalled at what he considered a disproportional penalty. The judge explained:

> The court believes that to sentence Mr. Angelos to prison for the rest of his life is unjust, cruel, and even irrational. Adding 55 years on top of a sentence for drug dealing is far beyond the roughly two-year sentence that the congressionally-created expert agency (the United States Sentencing Commission) believes is appropriate for possessing firearms under the same circumstances. The 55-year sentence substantially exceeds what the jury recommended to the court. It is also far in excess of the sentence imposed for such serious crimes as aircraft hijacking, second-degree murder, espionage, kidnapping, aggravated assault, and rape. It exceeds what recidivist criminals will likely serve under the federal "three strikes" provision. At the same time, however, this 55-year additional sentence is decreed by § 924(c)."

Just recently, after spending a decade in prison and having his case championed by many prominent advocates, Weldon's prosecutor reconsidered the sentence and worked with the judge to allow for his release—a shining but rare outcome.

Weldon's story gives us hope that we can make a difference even in the most egregious cases of disproportional sentencing when we choose to advocate for justice.

Reactionary lawmaking

As we discussed in Chapter Three, the War on Drugs and

mandatory-minimum sentencing contributed to a boom in the prison industry. Many of the people sentenced and imprisoned in the 1980s are still there today, serving excessively long sentences.

Many policymakers had good intentions for imposing stiffer and mandatory sentences during the '80s and '90s. They wanted to limit judicial discretion, promote sentencing uniformity, and curb what they viewed as unduly disparate and lenient sentences being handed down at the time. They were also responding to voters who were frightened and upset by an uptick in violent crime—often by people convicted of repeat offenses who were released from prison only to go out and commit another crime.

Outside groups, researchers, and citizens also called on legislators to mandate determinate sentences (meaning sentences that are fixed, allowing for less discretion by judges and less flexibility for parole). Some groups were motivated by a concern for procedural fairness, to correct racial inequities and unpredictability in sentencing, while others thought fixed and lengthier sentences would serve as a better deterrent and would put a stop to judges who were, in their view, being too lenient.

A good portion of the electorate also supported these reforms at the time. News reports of inner-city violence and increasing crack cocaine use frightened citizens. The harshest three-strikes law came about in California after the murder of Kimber Reynolds, 18, of Fresno, and the kidnapping and murder of Polly Klaas, 12, from the San Francisco Bay Area. Both young girls were killed by men with criminal histories fresh out of prison, where they'd been serving time for other similar, violent crimes. Shock and outrage dominated California news coverage for weeks on end and motivated voters to pass the three-strikes law via referendum in 1994. Under this law, people convicted of a third-time offense were given sentences of 25 years to life. California was unique in that it put the three-strikes law into place not just for violent crimes, but for any crime.

While this law got some people with violent convictions off the street, it also put away people who committed petty crimes.

Consider the case of Jerry Dewayne Williams. Jerry had a criminal history and had already served sentences for his past crimes. He was released from prison in April 1993, and according to news reports, he made excellent progress, finding a job and passing drug tests. Jerry appeared to be rehabilitated, so much so that his parole officer ended his parole in May 1994, ahead of schedule.

But that summer, Jerry went with friends to Redondo Beach in California. He ended up getting arrested for stealing a slice of pizza from some children.

Normally, petty theft would be categorized as a misdemeanor, which would carry a sentence of less than 18 months if he were convicted. But because of his past record and the three-strikes law, Jerry received a sentence of 25 years to life in prison.

Prosecutors alleged that Jerry had essentially bullied the group of 7- to 14-year-olds into sharing their food. Jerry defended himself, saying he asked politely and thanked the children afterward. One boy testified that Jerry frightened him, however, and that—along with the three-strikes law—helped to seal his fate.

Jerry's third strike could be elevated to a felony, regardless of severity. In this case, it was, thanks to his prior convictions. The justice system looked at his past and saw only his mistakes, not any progress he had made.

Jerry's public defender, Arnold Lester, pointed out that his client now faced the same sentence as someone convicted of rape, child molestation, or carjacking. Jerry would not be eligible for parole for 20 years. Even the judge believed the sentence was too harsh, but the three-strikes law demanded it.

Jerry shared a cell with a man convicted of murder who was serving a shorter sentence.

Eventually, Jerry was able to convince a judge to shorten his sentence and ended up serving about five years. Today he is free but faces the struggle that many people with felony records do—it's very hard to find a job, and if he were to be arrested, he would be back in prison for a long time. The progress he made seems to have been eroded.

Did Jerry Williams receive justice? To answer that question, we need to think about what the goals of the justice system are, and indeed, what we mean by justice in the first place.

When criminal justice policy comes from our fears and reactions to current events, rather than being based on enduring principles and evidence-based practices, it has unintended consequences. Those consequences include disproportional sentences, or alternatively, excessive uniformity, when mandatory sentences prevent judges from responding to the unique facts of each case. As judges have lost discretion, prosecutors have gained more authority over sentences. Prosecutors who decide what crime to charge a defendant with, and the charge they choose to bring, may come with the heavy burden of a mandatory-minimum sentence.

Critics of the criminal justice system point out that prosecutors are incentivized to win cases, sometimes above other priorities. If one individual's discretion can have such influence over the fate of an accused person, would it not be better to hand that discretion over to a judge, who ought to be impartial, than to the prosecutor, who will benefit from obtaining a conviction?

In addition to judicial discretion, should we consider the victim's perspective? If we value repairing relationships and validating those directly harmed under a restorative approach, should we also consider moving some discretion to victims, so long as there are proportional limitations? In other words, should a victim be able to play a more significant role in what sort and severity of punishment the person who harmed them should receive?

While it may be proportional to require a minimum amount of time served to satisfy what is owed for the harm to the victim, a restorative approach to justice may also allow for a sentence to be shortened when a prisoner can demonstrate that he or she has earned back the public's trust. This approach, called an earned-time credit, allows prisoners to earn days off their sentences for participating in certain prison programs and maintaining a record of good conduct. In addition to promoting a more constructive culture within prison, these policies send a message that making amends and earning back the public's trust are the expectation during incarceration. Earned-time policies, which provide a powerful incentive for participation in programs designed to reduce recidivism, can also increase the likelihood that prisoners will be prepared to reenter the community as law-abiding citizens.

Because many people in prison are serving unduly long sentences, and because of policies that will continue to add to their numbers, we need to think critically about how we can amend the system to promote proportional and restorative punishments.

The injustice of inconsistency

If we are going to talk about consistent and just punishment, we need to have a conversation about race. Why are minorities so greatly overrepresented in our prison population, and what we can do about it? Nationally, black people are incarcerated almost six times more often than white people, and Hispanics are more than twice as likely to be incarcerated as whites.

Police stop a higher percentage of black people than they do white or Hispanic people, according to a recent study. Hispanics and black people were also more likely to be searched than white people. Although national surveys show that rates of illicit drug use and drug dealing are roughly even across races, the rates of arrest for drug possession and dealing are significantly higher among black individuals. Controlling for differences in the facts of the case, black men receive harsher penalties than white men. The reasons for these disparities throughout the system are complex and sometimes a source of controversy. Rooting out these disparities often requires not just a change in the law, but also changes in cultural perceptions and underlying factors like poverty and other limits to opportunity. Nevertheless, we should critically evaluate where a change in the law can indeed bring about more just outcomes across racial lines.

For example, not that long ago, the sentencing disparity between offenses for crack and powder cocaine was 100:1. Crack and powder cocaine are different forms of the same drug. However, 85 percent of individuals arrested for crack cocaine are black. So, the 100:1 ratio resulted in vast racial disparities for comparable offenses. In 2010, at the urging of Prison Fellowship and many others, Congress passed the Fair Sentencing Act, which brought down the disparity. However, it remains at 18:1 today.

Race is not the only factor contributing to sentencing inconsistency. Sometimes, it's just a matter of where you are.

In the United States, someone can get a five-year sentence for smoking marijuana in one state, but someone in another state can engage in this same behavior on a perfectly legal basis. In Texas, 16- and 17-year-olds are automatically tried as adults, regardless of the crime, even though just across the state line in Louisiana, and in almost all other states, youth of the same age are handled in the juvenile system, where incarceration is far less likely. In New Jersey, stealing something worth just $200, well below the cost of an iPhone, will get you slapped with a felony, whereas Wisconsin sets the felony threshold at $2,500.

The great variance in the sentences we dole out for the same crimes, based solely on jurisdiction, should give us pause.

A call for reform and restoration

Congress and the states have begun to roll back many of the policies from the 1980s and '90s, but alternatives to incarceration remain underutilized. We should push our elected officials to think outside the bars.

Prison Fellowship's founder, the late Chuck Colson, wrote about his disappointment after meeting with legislators who felt that they had no choice but to respond to crime with massive prison-building projects in the late 1980s. He pointed out that in the Old Testament, Israel's most common means of punishment was restitution, or payment made directly to the victim. In the New Testament, the tax collector Zacchaeus promised to pay back anyone he had cheated fourfold. When restitution is ordered in Scripture, it is often for greater amounts than the direct cost of the theft or injury, taking into account the actual loss to the victim, such as lost wages.

Our current criminal justice system often does not utilize restitution and other alternatives to incarceration, such as drug, mental health, and veterans courts. Such courts can consider alternative programs that target the factors leading up to crime, including addiction, mental illness, post-traumatic stress, and other pernicious contributors. These alternatives advance retributive and utilitarian goals, reducing future offenses. They can also increase victim satisfaction and better serve relational or restorative justice that is emphasized in Scripture.

In the past decade, sentencing reforms have helped put a dent in the prison population, which peaked in 2009. However, these changes have often targeted less serious offenses or only provide exceptions to mandatory minimums, rather than overhauling the previous sentencing schemes. Christians should be at the forefront of the sentencing reform movement, demanding that punishment correspond to the seriousness of the offense, the responsible party's intent, and sentences imposed in similar cases.

Prison should be reserved for people who pose a true threat to the community. We should look to alternatives to incarceration, particularly for those with nonviolent offenses. A popular slogan, particularly among conservative supporters of justice reform, is, "We need to lock up people we're scared of, not the ones we're just mad at." However, the catchy phrase can send too simplistic a message that may unintentionally imply we can throw away the key when it comes to those with violent convictions. Even when someone needs to be incarcerated, we must still seek a proportional response, regardless of the type of offense. We should also remember that those who justly remain in prison, even for life, are still made in God's image, with great value in His sight. God can redeem and restore them, and even while serving their sentences, they can make meaningful contributions to their prison communities.

Many Christians on both sides of the issue feel strongly about whether the death penalty is a proportional and just punishment. Christian organizations and individuals with whom we partner have biblically based views both in support of and in opposition to capital punishment. For this reason, Prison Fellowship has deliberately decided to take no official position on the death penalty. Nevertheless, Prison Fellowship has a long history of convening Christian leaders for open dialogue on the death penalty. We encourage you to read up on the biblical arguments for and against the use of the death penalty as well as the current data on issues with its implementation. Prayerfully consider your response, as efforts to abolish or reinstate the death penalty may come to your state.

We believe law follows culture. In other words, elected officials take their cues from us, the people. Politicians have long used fear to pass tough-on-crime legislation. They do so because they think that's what their constituents want to hear or because our silence allows them to continue. But if we change the culture, we can change the law—and ultimately change the system.

In the last chapter of this book, we'll discuss how you can advocate for reform. It's easier than you might think. Although we hope you will seek to dive deeper, and Prison Fellowship is eager to equip you to do so, it can be as simple as donating your signature to an online petition.

For those policymakers who have been willing to champion justice reforms, we also need to offer encouragement. For this reason, Prison Fellowship launched the Faith & Justice Fellowship in May 2016. This bipartisan body includes members of Congress, governors, and state legislators motivated by their various faith traditions and committed to prioritizing and advancing restorative values in the criminal justice system. The members can share ideas and best practices on justice reform and build a growing movement of leaders who understand the enduring, values-based rationale for justice that restores.

Punishment in America today is complex and rapidly changing as we grapple with what is truly just and fair. Christians can and should play a role in advancing proportional sentencing and punishment that promotes restoration of communities, victims, and those responsible for crime.

Debi, whose story you read at the beginning of this chapter, now advocates for sentencing reform and justice that restores.

"I am now an advocate for all the grandmas, moms, and daughters I left behind," explained Debi in a 2015 hearing on sentencing reform legislation before the U.S. Senate Judiciary Committee. Will you join her?

Chapter Six

Justice That Listens:
What Do Victims Need?

During the year between college and law school, I (Heather) lived and worked in East Africa. One morning, I woke to strange noises from the second bedroom of my apartment. But my roommate was out of town—so who was banging around in her room?

Still groggy, I stumbled out of bed and saw a strange man rifling through my roommate's closet. I screamed at the top of my lungs and, without thinking, I ran at him. He fled through the balcony where he had entered—the door to which I had accidentally left unlatched the day before. I later found one of my bags pulled out from under my bed and realized that the man had been in my room while I slept! He had taken my cell phone. I soon realized that several of my roommate's possessions had been taken as well.

I called my phone from the landline in the apartment. Sure enough, an unfamiliar man answered. I was somehow calm. "God sees you," I told him. After I demanded his name several times, he hung up.

There is a good chance that you have been a victim of crime at some point in your life, whether someone pickpocketed your wallet on the subway, someone close to you abused you, or someone you loved died because a driver got behind the wheel drunk.

In 2016, an estimated 15.9 million households in America experienced property crime, while 5.7 million people reported being victims of violent crimes. Approximately 21 out of every 1,000 people over age 12 have been the victim of a violent crime, and 1.2 out of every 1,000 adolescents in the United States have been victims of a reported sexual assault. Advances in technology have made it possible for anyone to become a victim of crime without even leaving their home; in 2014, 17.6 million U.S. residents had their identities stolen. Many others have been victims of online scams or other forms of cybercrime.

Those numbers should outrage us. But even more outrageous is the fact that an estimated 3.3 million violent crimes go unreported every year. That's more than half of all violent crimes. Survivors of crime often avoid reporting what happened to them for many reasons, including:

- Fear of retribution
- Belief that the crime isn't important enough to report
- Denial or minimization of what happened as a coping mechanism

Even reported crimes are often left unresolved. About 41 percent of murders, 60 percent of rapes, and 87 percent of burglaries go unsolved each year. Victims of crime may feel that even taking the time and effort to tell their story to authorities will not bring them justice.

In this chapter, we will explore what it means to be a victim, how the criminal justice system has dealt with victims historically, and what we can do for victims of crime. Whether we are victims or not, we should be concerned with victims' rights and advocate on their behalf.

Who is a victim?

Exactly who qualifies as a victim? Broadly, a victim is someone impacted by a crime. But in the criminal justice system, the victim label is complicated.

Legally, a victim is defined as someone eligible for compensation, or someone given legal victims' rights, but that eligibility varies by state. Most states offer compensation or victims' rights only to victims of particular types of offenses, usually crimes of violence. A few, like California, offer victim status to victims of a much broader range of crimes.

The impact of less serious crimes (say, pickpocketing) can still be significant and lasting. When the criminal justice system fails to acknowledge that someone impacted by a misdemeanor or nonviolent crime is still a victim, it can add to the trauma of what happened.

What about the victim of murder? That person is no longer alive, but does his or her family have rights? Typically, in the case of murder, most states consider a parent, child, or spouse of a murder victim to be a victim as well, eligible for victims' rights.

In some states, immediate family members are also allowed to represent the victim if he or she is incapacitated, incompetent, or a minor. Each jurisdiction takes its own approach. Many allow only people with specified relationships to serve as the direct victim's representative.

We must also be aware of the needs of those who are victimized but not given that legal status. The impact of crime on extended family, friends, and neighbors can produce a never-ending ripple. A close friend of someone who is, for example, mugged or raped, can experience trauma, fear, and other effects, simply because of their relationship with the person.

David Hatch is an example of such a victim. His daughter, after a fight with her boyfriend, fled in her car. Her boyfriend allegedly followed in his car, chasing her. As she tried to evade him, David explains, she crashed her car and was killed. However, no charges were filed against anyone, since the daughter was driving her own car and there wasn't sufficient evidence to prove that her boyfriend caused her to crash or intended her to do so. David is a victim in many ways, but not recognized as such by the state.

The community at large can be victimized by crime, even if indirectly. If someone buys a home, and a few years later, people in the neighborhood start dealing drugs and committing other crimes, the homeowners are victims, even if they never interact with the people dealing drugs directly. The value of their property, now in a high-crime area, plummets, and they can't sell their house or must do so at a loss. Similarly, a child growing up in a neighborhood with a lot of crime, violence, and gang activity is likely to witness violence. Beyond that trauma, he may even turn to crime himself.

The government's limited view of a legal victim is just one example of how the modern criminal justice system is in some ways ill-equipped to meet the needs of people and communities harmed by crime.

Justice for victims

The criminal justice system is adversarial by design, often pitting defendants against the state and promoting "winning" over identifying the victim's needs and the responsible party's obligations. As we discussed in Chapter Two, the vast majority of defendants enter into a plea agreement with the prosecutor instead of going to trial. The prosecutor, who negotiates the plea deal, can consider a victim's opinions, but they don't have to do so. Some states have a right-to-confer law, which allows victims to discuss the case with the prosecutor. These dynamics bring tension and questions to the surface. When should the government's interest in an efficient justice system trump victims' rights? Should the victim, as the party directly harmed, have exclusive right to show mercy?

The point in the process at which victims can assert their rights is also a matter of debate. On one hand, some people argue that victims should not be present at a trial, positing that this makes it difficult to ensure the fairness of the proceedings. A defendant is presumed innocent until proven guilty. When a victim is in the courtroom, it's harder to maintain that presumption of innocence.

Alternatively, others have asserted that victims' rights should be considered even before a case comes to trial, during the investigation. Otherwise, the victim may lose any ability to weigh in on critical pre-charging decisions.

Our current justice system allows any victim of a crime to file a civil lawsuit, and some argue that the civil law provides remedy for victims and should be their primary recourse. However, that's not as easy as it sounds. Victims must navigate a complicated system by themselves or hire an attorney at their own expense— both of which keep some victims from even trying.

Victims' rights—a brief history

Although the justice system still needs reform, America has come a long way in recognizing and advancing victims' rights. In colonial America, there was no such thing as a public prosecutor. Victims had to take matters into their own hands, arresting the perpetrator and representing themselves. This probably led to some very interesting courtroom scenes! Of course, this meant that victims without means were also often without recourse. In 1704, the first public prosecutors were introduced. This continued until the eventual elimination of all private prosecutions around 1900.

The first national victimization studies, conducted in 1966, showed that victimization rates were much higher than reported by law enforcement. The findings raised the profile of the impact and reach of victimization and led to a national focus on victims' rights and needs.

The first crime victim compensation fund to assist victims with reimbursing expenses resulting from crime, started by California in 1965, grew into a nationwide network of state compensation programs. In the early 1970s, the first victim assistance programs were launched.

In 1981 President Ronald Reagan established a National Crime Victims' Rights Week, and in 1982, the President's Task Force on Victims of Crime released its report, outlining 68 recommendations that became the blueprint for many government policies and programs in existence today. The report recommended amending the Sixth Amendment of the U.S. Constitution to include victims' rights, such as the right to be present during trial and to be heard at critical stages in proceedings.

That recommendation never became law. Efforts to amend the U.S. Constitution have advanced through Congress but never reached the president's desk. Nevertheless, the task force's recommendation provided momentum for state constitutional amendments. Today, 33 states have victims' rights amendments in their state constitutions.

Generally, these include the right to:

- protection and privacy (including police escorts, restraining orders, witness protection programs, and relocation);
- information (about their legal rights and how to exercise them, and notice of criminal justice proceedings and the status of the perpetrator, including information about his or her incarceration, escape from confinement, capture, parole hearings, release, etc.);
- attend criminal justice proceedings;
- be notified of all court dates, sentencing, parole hearings, legal proceedings, and other relevant information about the defendant and the case;
- speak in court and other proceedings about the personal impact of the crime; and
- restitution or compensation.

After decades of progress to establish more robust victims' rights and services, lawmakers realized that many of those rights often were not enforced. In 2004, the Crime Victims' Rights Act (CVRA) was passed, giving victims standing at both the trial and appellate levels. It permits victims to retain an attorney. Since then, dozens of court decisions have been issued, helping to bolster the victim's role as a true participant in the criminal justice process.

Many states allow victims to write and read victim impact statements in court. Victim impact statements provide an avenue within the traditional criminal justice process for victims to share, in their own words, the harm they have experienced. Commonly given during sentencing, victim impact statements can also be issued at parole hearings and other points in the criminal justice process. Studies have shown higher levels of victim satisfaction and emotional recovery when victims are allowed to be involved in the criminal justice process, with victim impact statements being one of the most effective ways to include them in this process.

Restitution and compensation

In some cases, victims have the right to restitution or compensation. These terms are similar but not synonymous. Both are aimed at trying to make things right for victims, but both have severe limitations.

Restitution is monetary, in-kind, or other forms of amends due to the victim directly from the party responsible for the harm caused by the offense. The current criminal justice system generally only provides opportunities for monetary restitution. Unfortunately, even when the court orders restitution, it's often challenging for victims to receive it.

Imagine, for example, that a person robs a house. His motive? He wants to buy drugs, but he has no money of his own. He takes valuables, such as jewelry, and sells everything he steals for pennies on the dollar, just to get some cash, which he then spends on drugs. He eventually gets arrested, tried, and convicted. The robbery victim may have the right to restitution, and the court may order the defendant to pay it. However, the problem that motivated him to rob the house in the first place (his lack of financial resources to buy drugs) means that getting him to pay restitution is practically impossible. The jewelry is gone, scattered to various pawnshops or possibly sold and resold several times. Even the drugs are gone. Just as before, the person who committed the robbery has few, if any, financial resources. Add to this the fact that the person who committed the robbery is now incarcerated, and the chances of his paying restitution become extremely low. Even after release, he may struggle to secure employment that would enable him to pay restitution.

Government fines and fees can be another hurdle to payment, as they are sometimes collected from the defendant ahead of restitution payments. There is nothing left for the victim.

Compensation funds, on the other hand, are paid by the government to victims of certain qualifying offenses to cover out-of-pocket expenses and lost wages when restitution is not available.

In 1984, the Victims of Crime Act (VOCA) established the Crime Victims Fund to support the dozens of existing state compensation funds through federal criminal fines, penalties, and bond forfeitures. While compensation funds aim to meet the needs of victims who may not qualify for or be able to enforce restitution payments, the funds can be difficult for victims to access. In fact, some states and even the federal government have not been transparent about their use of these funds.

While millions of crimes are committed and reported each year, only a small fraction of eligible victims receive anything from victims' compensations funds. Why? Because even requesting funds is complicated. To be eligible for compensation, victims must have reported the crime to law enforcement within a designated time period, often no more than 72 hours. Specific documentation of the crime must be submitted. Survivors of crime sometimes fail to report what happened or don't do so immediately. They lack knowledge of compensation programs or may not realize they are eligible. They struggle to navigate the bureaucracy involved. As a result, few victims receive compensation.

In 2016, the VOCA Fund had a balance of around $9 billion at year end. Even though the law requires unused funds be retained in the fund for future victim services expenses, the federal government uses a portion of the balance as an offset against other federal government spending programs. Likewise, states have used victim compensation funds for purposes other than victims' services. For example, California lawmakers moved $18 million from its victim compensation fund to the general budget. Talk about outrageous!

Justice that restores

Victims of crime must navigate a difficult system that often exacerbates the trauma they have already experienced. We need a new approach to criminal justice, one that recognizes and advances the dignity of human life while promoting justice and restoring communities. Scripture clearly shows us God's concern for victims. As Christians, we have a responsibility to share that concern and act on it.

It is one thing to feel empathy for victims of crime, or to say that you "have a heart" for them. But justice that restores means we move beyond concern to action.

Justice that restores invites us to do two things: first, advocate for greater rights for victims, but also, on a more personal level, to reach out to victims of crimes and respond to their physical, emotional, financial, and spiritual needs.

Several faith-based ministries and churches are spearheading innovative responses to meet the needs of victims of crime. In 1988, Prison Fellowship piloted an initiative called Neighbors Who Care, rallying Christians to meet the physical needs of victims of crime, primarily people impacted by property crime. Neighbors provide transportation, repair property, and simply listen to people impacted by crime.

Inspired by the mission of the original Neighbors Who Care ministry, local victim ministries continue to find practical ways to assist victims. For example, Neighbors in Christ in Montgomery, Alabama, repairs doors that have been kicked in, fixes broken locks, and replaces shattered windows. They also transport domestic violence victims from their homes to new, safer locations.

Prison Fellowship International has created the Sycamore Tree Project, which brings together victims and prisoners for a facilitated discussion about crime and justice. Although the victims in the program are not the victims directly harmed by the participating prisoners, the forum provides the participants with an opportunity to learn about the impact of crime on victims. The project exists in dozens of countries across the world and has been shown to reduce the likelihood of reoffending among the prisoners who participate.

Elizabeth, whose mother was brutally attacked, suffered in "my own personal hell" for two years before she began participating in the Sycamore Tree Project. "The way the course chips away at the walls we have built around ourselves is quite amazing," she says. "It is truly based on honesty, trust, and respect. And the support we have shown each other has been heart-warming. For me personally, there has been a huge amount of healing."

Another program, Bridges to Life, invites victims to meetings with prisoners who are still incarcerated. Both the victims and the prisoners tell their stories. Just hearing a victim's story forces prisoners to face the reality of how their crime has hurt someone—and brings healing on both sides of the prison bars.

"That program did for me, and for the other guys I have seen go through it, what nothing else in prison could have done," said Lonnie Jones, who was imprisoned in Texas for a robbery gone wrong that resulted in the death of the homeowner. "There's no way you can just sit there and talk to someone that has been affected by crime, someone that has gone through something as traumatic as a rape or a loved one's murder—there's no way you can look them in the eyes and not be affected." Lonnie requested to participate in the Bridges to Life program several times and went on to become a facilitator before finally being granted his release from prison in 2009, 31 years after his arrest.

Victim-impact classes like the Sycamore Tree Project often occur after sentencing with unrelated victims and prisoners. Restorative justice programs, in which the victim and the person responsible for the harm develop an individualized restitution plan to make amends, can be used as an alternative to incarceration. The plans developed in such programs demonstrate that the path to making things right for victims can be incredibly individualized.

Danielle Sered is the executive director of Common Justice, a unique alternative-to-incarceration and victim-service program based in Brooklyn, New York. As part of the intensive, 15-month program, which includes supervision by the program and the court and a curriculum designed to decrease future violence, defendants in Common Justice are required to meet with the people they harmed in a restorative process and reach agreements about how to make things as right as possible. These agreements, which replace the prison sentences the defendants would otherwise have served, include school, work, restitution, community service, as well as agreements unique to each case.

Danielle describes how in one case, during a meeting between a man who had been robbed and the man who robbed him, the victim took up the responsible party's offer to teach him self-defense. This idea seemed puzzling to Danielle and her staff at first, but they made arrangements to follow through in a martial arts studio under trained supervision. The man who committed the robbery taught the man he had harmed techniques to break free from his grip, and, with practice, the victim mastered the skills. The next day, the victim called Danielle to express his excitement that "Nothing happened!" when he walked by a large man on the street. Since the robbery, the man had suffered common symptoms of trauma, his heart racing even when a petite older woman passed him from behind. The self-defense training, taught by the very person who attacked him, had restored his confidence and sense of safety.

Restorative justice programs have also proven effective at lowering recidivism rates and increasing victim satisfaction compared with the traditional criminal justice process. When a victim has a low sense of agency in the process, their satisfaction with the system decreases significantly. They may feel like they are being victimized a second time because they cannot control what is happening to them.

Mediation and restorative justice programs can give some of that autonomy back to the victim. Unlike the court system, these programs can give victims an opportunity to ask questions about the crime and the perpetrator's motivation. One study on mediation found that prior to meeting the person responsible for a crime committed against them, 23 percent of victims were afraid of being re-victimized by the person. After meeting them and talking about the offense and its impact on all involved, only 10 percent of victims were still fearful of being re-victimized.

These are encouraging examples, but there is still a need and great opportunity for Christians to support all victims of crime in their own congregations and communities.

Jesus' teaching on victim care

In Luke 10:25-37, Jesus tells the story of a Samaritan who comes across a robbery victim as he is traveling. Jesus tells the story for several reasons, primarily to answer the question, "Who is my neighbor?" However, the story also answers the question, "How should I respond to victims of crime?"

Jesus says we are to study the response of the Samaritan to this victim, and "go and do likewise."

What does the Samaritan do? First, unlike a priest and a Levite who pass this man by, the Samaritan takes notice of the victim and resists saying, "not my problem." Then he responds to the man's physical needs by bandaging his wounds. He also addresses his financial needs, taking him on his own transportation and paying for his care at an inn out of his own resources. Finally, he does not provide a one-and-done response. We know the Samaritan plans to follow up because he tells the inn owner, "When I return, I will reimburse you for any extra expenses."

The Good Samaritan parable provides a roadmap as we face victims' needs in our own congregations and communities. First, don't turn a blind eye. In some cases, friends may share they have been a victim of crime. However, others may not feel comfortable disclosing abuse, particularly domestic or sexual abuse that often is committed by close family or friends. We should pay attention to clues that perhaps someone needs our help, even if they cannot verbalize it.

Second, respond to the person's immediate needs. For example, some victims need help repairing their home after a burglary. If they have physical or financial needs you can meet, do so, or ask others in your church to partner with you. Responding also includes simply listening and validating the victim's experience.

The power of validation

When a crime happens, it can't be undone. No one can rewrite the story of what has already occurred. But supporting victims may help them move forward on their journey and perhaps even begin to heal them from the trauma. If a victim of crime is willing to share their experience with you, listen to their story and resist the urge to "fix" them or tell them you know how they feel. You don't have to respond with eloquent words or what you think are biblical answers. Oftentimes, that response does more harm than good. Usually the best way to help is simply to listen and to validate their story.

What is validation? In short, it's saying, "I'm so sorry that happened to you. It wasn't right. You've suffered an injustice." It might look like a simple conversation. For example, one day at Prison Fellowship headquarters, Heather told Jesse the story of the home invasion (which we shared at the beginning of this chapter), which had occurred five years prior.

Heather was telling this story to Jesse the way she often did, as a joke. She had never personally identified as a victim of crime, and in fact, told Jesse, "I've never been a victim of a crime, really. But there was this incident when I was living in East Africa. It was pretty funny, really. …" In the back of her mind, Heather felt responsible for not properly latching the door. In addition to her phone, some of her roommate's things had been taken. The man was never caught. She looked for him constantly for the rest of her year living abroad. The feeling of violation and lack of resolution remained. She used humor to cover up her conflicted feelings about the incident.

Looking seriously at Heather, despite her comic recounting of the incident, Jesse replied, "I'm so sorry that happened to you. You are definitely a victim of crime."

It was not until Jesse listened carefully to her story, five years after the incident, that Heather even saw herself as a victim of crime. His simple response validated her experience. Slowly, she felt more comfortable sharing that she sometimes had trouble sleeping in a hotel room alone. She didn't feel as much need to cover her distress about the incident with humor. The conversation also helped her to be more empathetic to other victims, and more passionate about advocating for them.

While each person's experience and response to crime is unique, psychological studies confirm common traits that result from the trauma of crime victimization. Understandably, a victim often wrestles with fear of re-victimization, feelings of helplessness, and lack of security. We don't want to exacerbate this trauma by placing partial blame on the victim. The Samaritan didn't respond by saying, "Well, why was this man traveling the notoriously dangerous road to Jericho alone?" Likewise, we shouldn't, for example, tell a person who was sexually assaulted that it was brought on by their clothing or whether they had a drink.

When you feel helpless to respond to someone who has been harmed by crime, don't underestimate how truly listening and validating someone's pain or fear can move them one step forward on their personal journey. It might even empower them to advocate on behalf of other victims. It might be just what they need to take the next step. Be ready to take that step beside them.

Walking with victims through the justice system

We should walk alongside victims as they navigate the criminal justice system. Victims first need to decide of whether to contact the police. As mentioned earlier, many crimes go unreported. There are victim service specialists who can advise victims and help them develop a safety plan. If they do contact the police or get involved in the criminal justice system, support them as they navigate that process, which is often confusing, lengthy, and does not always turn out the way a victim might hope.

Continue to validate victims who face these frustrations and partner with them to advance their rights in the system.

Walking with victims through the emotional journey

Allow victims to process at their own pace. This may involve a long-term process of healing, including deep anguish, confusion, fear, challenges, and emotional ups and downs. As with anyone who has survived a traumatic event or loss, there is no exact timetable or "right" way to recover.

Also bear in mind that justice that restores requires prayerful discernment, particularly when it comes to forgiveness. Some Christians, despite their good intentions, do more harm than good. We're so inspired when we hear of someone (especially a person of faith) being willing to forgive a person who harmed them, that we push all victims to follow suit. Think, for example, of the Amish community that immediately forgave Charles Carl Roberts IV, the man who shot 11 little girls in an Amish schoolhouse in 2006. The community's willingness to forgive made headlines and even inspired a movie. But not everyone is ready to forgive quite so quickly, and it is not because they are somehow deficient in character or faith. Healing takes time. At first, the wounds of tragedy are raw.

The June 2015 Charleston shooting at Emanuel African Methodist Episcopal Church resulted in the death of nine congregants, including Ethel Lance. Ethel's daughter Nadine Collier made a statement that shocked many as she stood in the courtroom at the bond hearing before the young defendant. "I forgive you. You took something very precious away from me. I will never get to talk to her ever again, but I forgive you and have mercy on your soul. You hurt me. You hurt a lot of people. If God forgives you, I forgive you." Her extraordinary words captured the public's attention and were replayed by news outlets across the country.

Other victims' family members, including Nadine's sister, Sharon Rischer, who were unable to embrace the same sentiment, were not met with the same fanfare. "My sister Esther and I have been pushed aside, and everyone has gathered around Nadine," Sharon shared in an interview with Time magazine.

We should aim to embrace all those who are hurting. We cannot neglect needs or push people aside because their grief does not conform to our expectations. We should ask the Holy Spirit for discernment and stay mindful that each victim is on a personal journey. Remember our duty to "mourn with those who mourn," as Romans 12:15 instructs.

We must also understand the difference between forgiveness and reconciliation. Forgiveness is letting go of the hurt, but reconciling is re-embracing the person who caused the hurt. Those are two different things. While some victims may choose to reconcile with the person who has wronged them, this may not be appropriate or safe. As we walk alongside victims of crime, we should respect the boundaries needed for long-term protection and restoration.

For example, consider Jane (not her real name). She was repeatedly abused by her brother when she was a child. Years later, even though Jane's mother knew about the abuse, she told Jane she was disappointed that she wasn't closer with this brother and didn't go out of her way to spend time with him. Jane felt misunderstood and frustrated. She had forgiven her brother. However, she had not reconciled with him completely. She still felt uncomfortable around her brother at times, and was protective of her own children, not letting them spend time alone with their uncle. Forgiveness does not mean acting as if the offense never happened. And it does not require full reconciliation.

Finally, let's be clear that forgiveness is not inconsistent with moral outrage against injustice, nor is it a compromise of justice. Christ first justified each of us through His death on the cross in order that we might be forgiven. God is outraged by injustice. Likewise, Christians should confront evil, including crime, and not excuse it. When we push people who are not ready to forgive, or demand reconciliation where healthy boundaries would preclude it, we thwart justice, rather than advocate for it. And even when someone does forgive, it doesn't mean we shouldn't take action against injustice, or not punish crime appropriately.

Advocate for change

A restorative approach to criminal justice recognizes that crime is not just an offense against the government; it damages the security and well-being of the victim and the entire community. In the current criminal justice system, the government and the defendant are the direct parties in an adversarial process, while the victim and the community are often treated as observers.

Yes, the state must represent the needs of society at large, but it should not overlook the primary needs and rights of crime victims and the community. Justice that restores includes working to promote accountability and transformation of the person responsible. It advocates for the government to serve as a facilitator of justice, rather than acting as a direct party.

We will move toward justice that restores when the government changes its approach, providing the victim with a meaningful role in the process and recognizing the community as the place for solutions. As we have discussed in previous chapters, victim-impact classes, mediation, and restorative justice programs can all provide meaningful opportunities for victims of crime to engage in the justice process. A restorative approach to justice would also prioritize restitution for victims above government fees and fines. Ideally, individualized restitution plans would include more than monetary forms of amends, agreed upon together by the victim and the responsible party. The government can engage the community by inviting community leaders, faith leaders, and nonprofit organizations to talk about what needs exist and what solutions have worked.

No matter how far the government has come in advancing victims' rights, there will always be needs that Uncle Sam cannot meet. We must stand ready to aid and comfort, but also to pursue justice in behalf of victims. Everyone who cares about justice, especially Christians, must continue to advocate.

We hope that you will take time to prayerfully consider your role in caring for victims in your congregation and community. If we can follow the example of the Good Samaritan by responding to the needs of those who are harmed by crime, we can serve as a reminder to many of the hope and comfort available through Christ, providing a glimmer of light in a dark place.

Chapter Seven

Justice That Transforms:
Why Do We Need a Constructive Prison Culture?

Nick, *whose story you read in the opening pages of this book, was convicted of armed robbery and sent to prison when he was 17. He survived by becoming more violent. Nick said prison did not rehabilitate him, but rather, hardened his heart.*

Three years into his prison sentence, Nick was told he was going to have to do more time in prison because of crimes, such as assault, that he'd committed while incarcerated.

"I remember that absolutely shattering my world," he says. "I was writing letters to my family, saying, 'I've changed.' I was telling myself that the only reason I was acting the way I am, the only reason I'm fighting, the only reason I'm hustling, I'm taking advantage of people, is because I need to survive in this environment. And it hit me: I've always done this. I've always blamed my actions on others and justified them. I tell myself I'm doing this because of this person, because I have to. For the first time in my life, I looked around and I was all alone, nobody to blame but myself, and I had to take a step back, and realize that something had to change or I was never going to get out of this prison."

Nick found an opportunity for change in a place he didn't expect: a faith-based dorm.

"I signed up for that for all the wrong reasons," he says. "I wasn't doing it for God, but I knew I could start over, that this was an environment where they were talking about a release, talking about when you get out, so it was not just living for the day, but living for the future. And that was something I was interested in."

Nick was taken to a nearby prison that had the exact same layout and design as the prison he'd transferred from. It looked familiar, he says, "until I walked into the dorm, and at five in the morning there were 250 men sitting there. I had no idea why they were awake. Why were they up so early in prison? But they all had a Bible in their hands. They were all sitting down reading the Bible. And I said, 'Something's different here. This makes no sense to me.' That's when I noticed: this was no longer a prison culture, this was a culture of transformation."

Nick attended classes as part of the faith-based dorm program. Volunteers would come to lead Bible studies and get to know the prisoners. Two volunteers stood out to Nick: Simon and Corinne, an elderly couple from a small farming community in Pella, Iowa.

"I could never forget them. I would watch them walk 200 yards across the prison yard to come into the classroom with us once a week. I finally asked them, 'What are you two doing here? Why do you come in here?' Corinne's response was, 'Because we love you.' And I'm thinking, 'You don't know me, I have not had the opportunity to earn your love. What are you talking about?' And she said, 'Christ died for us before we were ever born, and I loved you before I ever met you.' Talk about transformed culture. That is the love of Jesus represented in somebody's life. Now, these words in this book, this holy book ... now these words had meaning, and they had action, and it penetrated my heart."

Nick was changed by his relationship with these faithful volunteers, who continued to show up and remind him that he mattered to God, and to them. He says their faithful presence, combined with their kind words, changed his life.

"From that, I took a step back: I do have value, I do have a purpose, I do have a calling, and it is not to sit in prison," Nick says. "That culture was brought in because the Simons and Corinnes of this world were willing to come in and spend time with me and tell me that Jesus loves me. That started this burning passion in my heart to be a part of that same process."

One week after release, at age 24, Nick began working in prison ministry. He now spends his time going into prisons, working with men and bringing them the message that Simon and Corinne brought to him.

"I know the value that they have. I know that God wants so much more for them," Nick says. "We spend time investing in these men's lives, and changing that culture, saying, 'You are so much more than this. You are not created to be a criminal. You were not created to be a sinner. Instead, you are a child of God. You are no longer going to be represented by your number, but instead you're going to be represented by your God.'"

Prison is a world all its own. In some ways, prison is like a nation-state, with its own borders, language, and culture. The most obvious characteristic is its borders, usually a fence or a wall, topped with razor wire. Perhaps not so obvious are the other two characteristics: language and culture.

The words and phrases that are unique to prison help to set it apart from the rest of society. For example, here is a statement that would make sense to most people in prisons across the country, but unless you have been to prison, you may have difficulty understanding it:

> "Man, my cellie shoots a kite every 20 minutes. The COs are fed up. He's only doing a nickel—I can do that standing on my head. He'll probably check in to PC because he is already late paying back soups and shots at two for one. He thinks he's a shot caller, but he's just a cell soldier. I'm just waiting for the yard to open so I can hit the iron pile and get my money, go to pill line, and stop messing with this lame fish."

Now, here is the same statement, translated:

> "My roommate sends a note to the administration every 20 minutes. The correctional officers are getting tired of dealing with him. He is only in prison for a five-year sentence, which is nothing. He will probably ask to go into protective custody (an isolation cell) because he is late on paying back ramen noodles and coffee that he borrowed—he will have to pay back two for each one that he borrowed. He thinks he is tough, but he only talks tough when we are in the cell. I'm waiting for the common area to open so I can go lift weights, get a good workout in, and get my medication. I can't wait to stop talking to this naïve, new guy."

Prison slang has variations depending on geographic location, but it is a defining characteristic of prison life. And it's more than just a way of talking. It reinforces the truth that prison is a place that's different—and a place that is generally not preparing people to reenter society when they get out.

Language is just one element of culture. Prison culture is unique, and for the most part, it's negative. Prison culture can make it harder for people to change their mindsets and their behaviors and can be exhausting for those who are looking to change the trajectory of their lives.

Culture is driven by values. It reflects what matters most to the people within that culture. For example, we don't tolerate stealing as a society because we value personal property rights, and we don't tolerate murder because we value human life. In prison, the values that drive the culture are, in many cases, antithetical to the cultural norms that we want people to abide by upon release.

For example, we value honesty as a society, but in prison, honesty can be viewed as a weakness. Once released, people are encouraged to network and make new relationships, but in prison, you don't talk to people unless you know them or are introduced. In society, we value trust, but in prison trusting people, even people in authority, can get you hurt. It's nonsensical to expect people who have lived by prison norms to shift to a completely different set of values simply because they have left that environment.

A violent culture

No one drifts into a positive culture. In fact, the culture in a prison can easily become violent and corrupt. Consider the Baltimore City Detention Center. Built before the Civil War, it had overcrowded, dank, dirty cells, unreliable plumbing, and a frightening culture. The jail serves as a chilling example of what can happen if a prison culture is left unchecked.

The jail, which housed men for up to 18 months, often awaiting trial, was largely run by a prison and street gang. In fact, many of the correctional officers employed by the jail were cooperating with the gang leaders.

In 2013, authorities broke up a smuggling ring inside the jail that was led by the notorious Black Guerilla Family gang. Thirteen female corrections officers were among those indicted. You read that right. The gang had such control of the jail that employees were smuggling in cell phones, drugs, cigarettes, and more, which they gave to gang leaders to be sold to other prisoners. As if that's not enough, gang leader Tavon White had impregnated *four* of the female corrections officers and given them lavish gifts purchased with the money they'd helped him make. Two of the women, while employed at the jail, had "Tavon" tattooed on their bodies.

Two years later, Maryland Governor Larry Hogan closed the jail and moved the prisoners to other locations. The closure was the right thing to do and has improved the situation, but such a toxic culture, even if dispersed, requires constant vigilance.

What do we mean by "constructive culture"?

So, what, exactly, is a constructive prison culture? The culture at the Baltimore jail was obviously not constructive. We know chaos, crime, and corruption are hallmarks of a destructive culture. But what does the opposite culture look like? A constructive prison culture, like the one Nick witnessed, mimics the cultural norms of a positive, productive society. It is a culture that facilitates good citizenship and encourages lasting, positive behavior changes.

The fruits of the Spirit—love, joy, peace, forbearance, kindness, goodness, and self-control (Galatians 5)—align perfectly with advancing constructive culture. We also know that, when it's lived out, the Gospel results in community and culture change. So, as Christians, we should see prisons as a perfect place to sow the values of God's Kingdom.

You have probably seen television shows that depict life behind bars, or that highlight the depravity present within the criminal justice system. Oddly, we seem to accept this as inevitable. We seem willing to allow our prisons to operate in a way that perpetuates criminality. This is rarely talked about, but it's outrageous. What if our health care system were allowed to function in a way that made people sicker? Or what about a school system that decreased literacy? Why do we tolerate failure when the safety of our community is at stake—not to mention the valuable human lives we waste when the system gives them little opportunity for transformation?

That doesn't make sense. As Christians, we have an opportunity to advocate for change not only in the laws that send people to prison, but also for change of the culture within prisons—because, with 95 percent of prisoners coming home, it profoundly impacts the culture outside of prison, too. We need to adopt a community-building mindset and begin to see our prisons as part of our larger community and, for those in the Body of Christ, part of our spiritual community.

Building a new culture

Constructing a prison culture that is consistent with the positive norms of a civil society is paramount to protecting communities outside of prison and achieving the greatest return on our investment in the criminal justice system. We allow our prisons to function according to a set of values that are inconsistent with civil society and, yet, we expect people to succeed once they pass the prison threshold.

The truth is that we have a justice system that doesn't seem to have the same accountability as our other government institutions. More than two-thirds of the people who are released from prison will go back through its revolving doors within three years.

Between federal and state government and nonprofit organizations like Prison Fellowship, America has spent billions of dollars on rehabilitation efforts inside prison walls. Yet, this investment loses its impact when it is in an environment that is not conducive to positive change. We can spend all the money, time, and resources in planting good seed, but if there is no sunlight, we can't expect it to grow.

How can the Church, the "light of the world," provide the sunlight needed to give the seeds that we plant the best chance to grow?

First, it is important that we understand that building a culture must go beyond holding church services or evangelizing people in prison. Once someone has accepted the Gospel, then what? This is certainly the beginning, but as the Church, we need to expand our expectations from counting hands raised and eyes closed to long-term, total transformation. We have heard people say that they stopped going to prison ministry meetings because they were always told the same message: "You need Jesus to save you from your sin." This message is true and important, but how do we introduce people in prison to the full Gospel message that impacts every aspect of one's heart and life? How can we help equip men and women in prison to be culture changers in their own unique context?

The Church must promote a prison culture that provides the best greenhouse for change—not just positive change for those who are in the family of God, but change that inspires all those around us. We want to see all people come to the saving knowledge of Christ. We want people who are in prison to have the opportunity to practice good citizenship before they return to the community. We provide that opportunity by countering the current cultural values that exist within our prisons, like suspicion, violence, and deceit, and promoting the values of trust, peace, and honesty. We encourage men and women behind bars to take responsibility for their past, make amends to those they have harmed, and take action to earn back the public's trust.

Prison Fellowship works toward the goal of a more constructive prison culture in a number of ways. In addition to our evangelistic Hope Events, in-prison Bible studies, and Prison Fellowship Connection Classes™ on a variety of topics, we've also had the opportunity to establish the Prison Fellowship Academy®, a long-term, intensive program that holistically addresses the roots of criminal thinking and behavior by providing a pro-social community atmosphere and opportunities for participants to practice the values of good citizenship. Present in more than 80 correctional facilities, the Academy instills practical knowledge and values based on a Christian worldview. Participants are prepared to be good citizens in their communities, whether they remain in prison or are released. As men and women leave prison, Prison

Fellowship provides referrals to local programs and resources on the outside to help them succeed.

Our most robust Academy programs allow participants to live together in a prosocial community. These units have a completely different culture than the typical prison culture because we talk about and reward values, including productivity, restoration, integrity, and responsibility, that will help men and women become good citizens.

Culture-building must be intentional. Nothing left to itself will yield a positive investment; in fact, it does the opposite, as we saw in the example of the Baltimore City Correctional Center. We can't expect good things to occur by warehousing people in prison and then forgetting about them. We must be proactive, and the Church can play a vital role in this process.

We're seeing culture change happen in the Prison Fellowship Academy sites across the country. We're seeing lives change through our programs and classes. To reach more prisoners and change the culture in more prisons, we need more volunteers to respond to the biblical invitation to visit those in prison. When more churches and individuals decide to join us in sharing the outrageous love of God with prisoners, we will see even more prisons and lives transformed as a result.

Building pathways to reconciliation

To have the greatest impact on prison culture, we must also seek to influence affected families and prison systems, rather than just individuals. There are probably people in your congregation who have a loved one in prison. Just as we are to "remember the prisoner," we should also remember those they have left behind. Having a loved one in prison can be a very difficult and lonely experience, particularly for children. We can walk alongside families, offering emotional and practical support.

Each Christmas season, through collaborations with local churches and community organizations that partner with Prison Fellowship's Angel Tree program, hundreds of thousands of children receive a gift and the Gospel message on behalf of their incarcerated parents. Angel Tree provides pathways for incarcerated parents to restore and strengthen relationships with their children and families.

Founded in 1982 by a former prisoner who witnessed firsthand the strained relationship between prisoners and their children, Angel Tree has grown to become the largest national outreach to the 2.7 million children of prisoners. Our partner churches also meet the physical, emotional, and spiritual needs of both children and families through year-round ministry, such as Angel Tree Camping®, Angel Tree Sports Clinic, and mentoring.

Caring for prisoners' families on their behalf plants seeds in their hearts. We can then cultivate those seeds by developing genuine relationships with men and women behind bars, inviting them to participate in programs within the prison walls.

The Gospel changes culture

The Apostle Paul understood that the Gospel can change culture—even prison culture. In Acts chapter 16, Paul and Silas find themselves in prison after casting a demon out of a woman fortuneteller. Let's pick up in verse 25:

> About midnight Paul and Silas were praying and singing hymns to God, and the other prisoners were listening to them. Suddenly there was such a violent earthquake that the foundations of the prison were shaken. At once all the prison doors flew open, and everyone's chains came loose. The jailer woke up, and when he saw the prison doors open, he drew his sword and was about to kill himself because he thought the prisoners had escaped. But Paul shouted, "Don't harm yourself! We are all here!"

Through Paul and Silas' influence, the prison culture changed. How? When the prison doors flew open, the guard was about to kill himself because he faced swift, painful retribution from his superiors if any prisoners were subsequently found to have escaped. But because Paul and Silas had already started to influence the other prisoners, they were able to say, "Don't harm yourself! We are all here!" They did not adhere to the cultural norm of escape. This is transformation in action.

We do not have information that the other prisoners were saved through Paul and Silas' interaction, but their values changed. This change, even if it was for a moment, saved the life of the prison guard. This is the impact a culture change can have on the prison environment. By providing a place for biblical values to flourish, we increase the safety inside prison and allow men and women the opportunity to adopt a new, positive way of life.

The Bible is full of stories of people God used to have a dramatic impact on culture, and consequently saved people's lives or rescued them from disaster. Joseph, for example, was able to influence Egypt to help prepare for a coming famine and save millions of lives. Esther influenced King Xerxes and saved her people from death. Other Christ-followers, like Martin Luther King Jr., have dramatically shifted the values of our society and have led sweeping cultural reform.

The Greeks understood the importance of culture. The word "apostle," which the Bible uses to describe someone who goes out to preach the Gospel, comes from the Greek word *apostolos,* which referred to a ship on a military expedition that was filled with colonists and all the culture of Greece. The historian Josephus uses this word to also describe a group of colonists going out on a mission.

This is our calling as the Church: not to just plant seeds, but to consider "visiting the prisoner" an extended discipleship relationship that can transform a culture. We need to create an atmosphere that allows people in prison to practice their faith, not just make a one-time decision.

We believe God has called Prison Fellowship to facilitate this kind of culture change in prisons. Through dedicated field staff and thousands of volunteers, we help create positive communities within prisons all over the country. These communities begin to live by a different set of values and take an active role in changing their culture. This goes beyond our Bible studies or the Academy. We also encourage and train prison staff and leaders, who can be some of the most powerful forces for positive change inside the walls.

The person who has the greatest opportunity to influence the culture in a prison is often the warden. Through Prison Fellowship's Warden Exchange® program, we work to bring prison culture transformation not just from the bottom up, but from the top down.

This innovative program provides leadership training for wardens and allows them to learn from one another. Incorporating weekly video conference and in-person residencies, the Warden Exchange convenes prison leaders from across the country for intensive training in best practices from some of the brightest thought leaders in criminal justice, law, business, and education. Participants graduate from the program with individualized action plans to bring restorative change to their facilities and build a safer, more rehabilitative prison culture.

Prison Fellowship's evangelistic Hope Events, Connection Classes, Bible studies, mentoring, Academy, and Warden Exchange don't just help those who are directly involved. If enough people in the prison participate, we hit a tipping point where they begin to impact the entire prison. We have seen reports of misbehavior for entire prisons with a significant Prison Fellowship presence drop significantly. People who are not in our programs, but in the same prison, begin to associate with program participants, and prison staff mention the visible difference in the way prisoners behave and interact.

Transformation and restoration are central teachings of the Gospel. For that transformation to occur, we must allow men and women in our prison system an environment conducive to growth. We want to offer a culture that will afford people the best chance to live up to their God-given potential, both while they're in prison and once they return to society. It's a daunting challenge and an exciting opportunity.

Chapter Eight

Justice That Redeems:
How Can We Unlock the "Second Prison"?

Robbie Robinson had been in and out of detention centers and prisons since he was 14 years old. During his second stint in prison, he had the opportunity to be a part of a Prison Fellowship program that prepared him for reentry.

"When I got out, I had hope because I had a lot of support in my back pocket. My mentor came and picked me up from prison. I didn't go back to where I 'fell from,' the town where I was arrested; I went to a whole new community," Robbie says.

With his mentor's help, he was able to get a job, join a church, and live in a transitional home.

"I was invited to speak at a corporation to share my story," Robbie says. "The owner of the company believed in me because he heard my story, and he wanted to give me a chance. They offered me a welding job there for 14 bucks an hour, and I never even filled out an application."

Robbie was the first former prisoner to work for this corporation. The owner told him, "You will be like the guinea pig. How you do within our company can open a big door for other individuals who have been in your situation, getting out of prison." Robbie saw this as his golden opportunity. He worked there for 10 years and was repeatedly promoted. That company now employs more than 300 people who have been in the prison system.

As he got his life back on track, Robbie married and had a son. When his son was in preschool, Robbie volunteered to assist at a school Halloween party.

School policy for volunteers included running background checks. That check revealed Robbie's felony conviction from years before. The school called Robbie's wife (not him) and told her he could not volunteer.

"That was when I felt the most judged—at my son's school," he says.

Robbie called the school superintendent and the principal and calmly but firmly asked for an explanation. He had come to school often to have lunch with his son but was now being denied the opportunity to volunteer.

"That's not who I am today," he told the administrators. "That was 15 years ago. I've been off parole since 2007." He had been out of prison for 10 years.

Because of his persistence, the school ended up apologizing and allowing Robbie to volunteer in his son's classroom.

"You can't keep persecuting people for what they've done in their past. I have paid my debt to society. I paid my money— everything I owed them. I've given them everything they wanted. I've done everything from society's standpoint just to be a full citizen in the United States. What more do you want?" Robbie says. Today, he runs a reentry center in his town to help others to become productive citizens. He understands firsthand the struggles that formerly incarcerated people go through and is trying to help people truly be free.

As we have seen throughout this book, the size and scope of America's criminal justice system has exploded over the past 40 years. Because of the over-criminalization and harsh sentencing we discussed in earlier chapters, roughly 70 million people in the United States have a criminal record. That's right—one in three adults has been arrested!

Most of the recent national conversation about criminal justice reform has focused on reducing the size of the prison population. But none of that touches on another problem: the long shadow of a criminal record. What happens when people come home? What role can they play in society? Those are vital questions. Ninety-five percent of people now incarcerated will be released one day, at a rate of more than 600,000 per year. They get out from behind bars, but are they truly free?

Justice often falters at the prison gate. While technically no longer behind bars, those leaving prison often find themselves severely restricted in many ways. Sometimes, these restrictions make sense: a person convicted of abusing children cannot get a job as a daycare worker, for example. Certain boundaries are appropriate for society and for the person convicted of a crime. But other times, the restrictions prevent people from starting a new life and becoming a productive member of their community. Even when people returning from prison are part of a reentry program and have a mentor and help along the way, as Robbie did, they can still run into barriers that far outlast the actual sentence for their crime.

Reentering the community after being incarcerated is a jarring and often difficult experience. Some people have a family and a home waiting, but many must build a life from scratch; housing, employment, transportation, community, identification, and more must be obtained. Former prisoners must go from an institutional environment, in which initiative and decision-making are discouraged, to one in which countless decisions must be made daily, each having lasting consequences.

Those who have served long sentences come out into a world that has been transformed by technology. Think how much the world has changed in the years since smartphones were introduced. Those who have been away for 10, 20, or more years are unfamiliar with the technological processes that dominate how we hunt for jobs, access services, or even pump gas. For them, coming out of the prison gates can feel as disorienting as time travel.

Every person has God-given potential and value. In a society where justice truly restores people, the payment of one's debt should be followed by an opportunity to regain trust and contribute to the community. That's not usually the case in America. Even if someone has worked hard to meet this challenge—if they have stayed clean and sober, met all the conditions of their release, served their time and paid their restitution—more obstacles await. Currently, there are more than 44,000 documented legal barriers and restrictions on people with a criminal record. Along with the unwritten social stigma attached to a criminal history, these restrictions affect all areas of life. Like a net that scoops up every kind of fish, these restrictions are often applied broadly, with little regard to whether they promote public safety. At Prison Fellowship, we call this troubling reality "the second prison."

Throughout our history, we have added more and more blanket restrictions to people reentering community, rather than assessing people's risks and potential on a case-by-case basis. Employers and landlords run quick internet searches to determine if applicants have ever become entangled with the criminal justice system. If they have been, they will often be excluded on that basis, regardless of whether they have already paid their debt to society. Many insurance companies even require that employers and landlords conduct these background checks, threatening to rescind coverage from those who don't comply.

The obstacles of the second prison extend beyond just jobs and housing. Someone with a criminal record, even if the crime was minor or committed long ago, may even find themselves barred from coaching their child's sports team, becoming a foster parent, obtaining professional licensing, or volunteering at the local juvenile detention center. This may even impact a person's right to vote. Being allowed to cast your ballot in the voting booth is one of the most fundamental rights in a democracy, yet more than 6 million men and women are not allowed to vote based solely on the fact that they have a criminal record.

Many of these restrictions clearly have little to do with public safety. In Colorado, you can't call a bingo game (or even help call one) if you've been convicted of a felony. New York applies a similar restriction to anyone convicted of any crime—no matter how minor. If you live in Michigan and have been convicted of a felony in the past decade, you can't have a dog that's part wolf. If you live in Louisiana and need money for college, you had better not have anything worse than a traffic ticket in your past. Students with a record are barred from receiving state-based financial aid from many programs. Some states block any person with a criminal record from becoming a barber, hair stylist, cosmetologist, manicurist, or massage therapist. When these restrictions are unrelated to people's crimes, they make it unnecessarily hard for them to function in society, or to provide for themselves and their families.

For people returning to their communities, the long-term effects of the second prison are deeply discouraging. For society, this situation is counterproductive. Stable housing, steady employment, and a feeling of belonging to the community all help people to stay out of prison for good. While there is never an excuse for crime, being denied eligibility for housing, moved to the bottom of the résumé pile, and turned away from the voting booth build up feelings of frustration and exclusion, making old addictions and behaviors seem more attractive. While some restrictions are necessary, the clear majority of these restrictions are not directly related to the crimes of which people have been convicted, and there is no relief from their lifelong punitive effects.

The prevailing negative stereotypes about people with a criminal record are also an important part of the second prison. People in the criminal justice system are often portrayed in television shows and news media as incapable of lasting change, if not downright monstrous. This perception creates a reality that keeps people in the margins of our society long after their debt has been paid. The second prison also has significant costs for society. In addition to the ongoing costs of prosecuting and incarcerating people who commit new crimes, it is estimated that the United States loses more than $78 billion per year in economic output because of the diminished economic potential of people in the workforce who have a criminal record.

Not everyone deserves a second chance to walk the streets. But people who are released, and who have paid their debt to society, deserve a fair opportunity to regain the public's trust and make a significant contribution to their families and communities. A former prisoner who is now a pastor once told us, "I'm not asking for any handouts, but I just don't want anyone to stand in my way." But this is what our culture often does—we stand in the way of opportunities for success.

We recently met a 72-year-old man in Minnesota who was interested in volunteering at a local hospice center. He filled out the application but quickly learned that he was denied because of a drug conviction when he was 22. He was denied the ability to volunteer because of a conviction that was half a century old! Perpetual punishment in America has undermined the biblical values of proportional punishment and redemption and has imposed second-class citizenship on millions of our family members, church members, neighbors, and friends. Are we really willing to let our society function this way?

In the musical *Les Misérables*, men who are in prison sing the following lines, "Look down, look down, don't look 'em in the eye. Look down, look down, you're here until you die," while Jean Valjean (prisoner 24601, who is about to get released), and Javert, a police inspector, have the following dialogue:

> Javert: Now, prisoner 24601, your time is up and your parole's begun; you know what that means.
>
> Jean Valjean: Yes, it means I'm free!
>
> Javert: No! Follow to the letter your itinerary. This badge of shame you'll show until you die.

Victor Hugo wrote the novel on which the musical is based in 1862, and the situation has remained the same for too long. It's time to eliminate barriers that prevent renewed, redeemed people from contributing to their communities. Individuals and their families deserve an opportunity for a second chance, and we should help them unlock it.

Proportional punishment, creating a constructive prison culture, and providing adequate reentry services are all necessary components to building a better criminal justice system, but we lose the return on our investment if we do not allow the millions of men and women who have been through the criminal justice system to ever be free from the stigma and collateral consequences of a criminal conviction. We seem to believe that people can change, but we are not settled on what changed people should be allowed to do. This is where Christians need to step up and be countercultural, exercising wisdom and compassion as they offer opportunities, support, and mentoring to those leaving prison.

What does research say?

A key issue in the criminal justice conversation is recidivism, or the rate at which people, once released, commit another crime and return to prison. However, there is very little focus on people who do not commit another offense after their release. It is assumed that everyone who committed an offense poses an indefinitely high threat of committing another one. But what if that assumption is incorrect?

The common cultural perception of people in the criminal justice system makes employers, landlords, and the state leery of extending them second chances. However, this fear is not based on facts. For example, a Harvard sociologist studied the service records of people who enlisted in the Army under a waiver that allowed them in despite having a felony conviction. Surprisingly, these individuals were, on average, no more likely to get kicked out than their peers, and they were promoted faster and to higher levels.

Another report commissioned by Prison Fellowship found that many people who committed crimes reach a point where their likelihood of committing another offense is equal to that of the general population. This finding, called "risk convergence," indicates that formerly incarcerated individuals who do not reoffend over a certain amount of time return to the same risk as the general population. The longer they go without reoffending, the better their chances of not doing so. The report, citing research done by Alfred Blumstein and Kiminori Nakamura, describes three variables that affect the risk convergence timeline for a specific person who committed an offense.

The first variable is the age of the person who committed the offense. The younger the individual, the longer it takes to reach a point of risk convergence. A 21-year-old who commits the same crime as a 35-year-old will take longer to have their risk of reoffending converge with the general population.

The second variable is violence. When someone commits a violent crime, it takes longer for their risk level to come down.

The third variable is whether it was a first offense. People who commit multiple offenses may take much longer to reach risk convergence. They've built a pattern of behavior that is harder to break.

The graph below shows the probability of arrest for someone who committed a burglary at age 16 and the probability of being arrested for an average member of society. Within four years, the risks become the same. And after that, the risk of re-arrest continues to be *slightly less than* the risk of arrest for the general population.

Probability of Rearrest

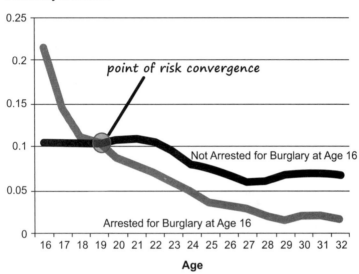

If we are going to treat people differently based on fear that they will recidivate, we should at least treat people according to the actual risk they pose to society. But we often miscalculate that risk. Suppose two 23-year-olds apply for the same job. One committed burglary as a teenager (with no further criminal convictions), and the other did not. Statistically, the 23-year-old with a criminal history is no more likely to commit a crime than the other job applicant against whom she is competing. But a background check run by the employer won't accurately reflect the real risks.

While the data say the risks converge, most employers and even lawmakers don't acknowledge that truth. Once someone has committed a crime, they can't erase it. Their offense follows them around, even though they have successfully reintegrated into society and refrained from committing more crimes.

When people reenter society, we should facilitate their success whenever it does not directly compromise public safety. We cannot work for justice while they are in prison, but then let our efforts falter once they are released.

Blocking people's ability to find housing and employment because of their past makes it hard for them to return to an honest way of living. Whenever individuals start to move beyond their offense, societal restrictions remind them that they cannot ever really outrun it. Like Jean Valjean, they face a world where their past haunts them, and people do not believe they've actually changed.

What does the Bible say?

What does the Bible tell us about the second prison?

When we look to Jesus, we see how He redeemed and elevated people that others convicted and condemned. He professed the unfaltering power of redemption in their lives. Think of Zacchaeus, the tax collector, considered a sinner by the people (Luke 19:1-10). When Zacchaeus shows he has changed and is making amends by giving possessions to the poor, Christ responds by saying, "Today salvation has come to this house, because this man, too, is a son of Abraham." When the criminal dying on the cross next to Jesus asks for Him to remember him, Christ responds by saying He will see him in paradise (Luke 23:32-43).

As Christians, we know that the Gospel changes people, but do we believe that changed people can, in turn, change people, communities, or even nations? We love the redemption stories of Moses and Paul—both of whom had blood on their hands—but are we willing to challenge the cultural barriers that would make us think twice before welcoming either of those men into positions of leadership today? Will you join us in meeting the challenge?

We hope at this point you are asking, "What can I do to help those caught in a second prison?" We'll explain more about how you can advocate for second chances in the next chapter.

Chapter Nine

Justice That Responds:
A Call to Act Justly and Love Mercy

I (Jesse) grew up in Southern California, in what you'd call Bible-Belt suburbia. I attended private Christian schools, went to church multiple times a week, and was the best at memorizing Bible verses. I could whip anyone at Bible "sword drills." I excelled in school and was good in sports. By any objective standard, I was a good kid.

I graduated high school with no ambition or purpose. I rejected the Christianity of my parents, which didn't seem to give me answers to the questions I was asking. I wrestled with the "whys" of life: Why is there pain? Why is there happiness? What is the purpose of life? Most of these are existential questions that many new high school graduates wrestle with, but I internalized more than most.

Ultimately, my internal pain drove me to thoughts of suicide, and I found myself looking in the mirror with a loaded .38 pressed in my mouth. By the Lord's grace, I didn't pull that trigger, but I shifted my pain into the pursuit of pleasure. Eventually, I took that same gun and robbed a bank at gunpoint. I was 21.

I had never been in the criminal justice system, so I had many lessons to learn. Like others whose stories you've read in this book, I learned them quickly and sometimes painfully.

Eventually, again through God's grace, I found myself in a Prison Fellowship in-prison program where I was confronted with a God that I had not met in all those years of church. Through some long conversations and much reading, I concluded that there was a God, and I wasn't Him. This changed everything.

I left prison after nearly eight years with a newfound purpose and vision. I graduated with honors with a bachelor's degree from Moody Bible Institute while I was still in prison, and I began studying for the Law School Admission Test in my prison cell.

I realized that I could make a difference and give back. I had grown to appreciate the rule of law and the legal process. I wanted to help others by becoming a lawyer. I enrolled in law school, served as president of the law school's honor council, graduated magna cum laude, and passed the Virginia bar exam.

To determine if I was morally fit to get my law license and practice law, I had to undergo several hearings where I provided multiple witnesses and answered any questions about my past criminal record.

Ultimately, that process took five years, ending in the courtroom of the Virginia Supreme Court, where I was denied a law license in a 4-3 decision. I'll never forget when one of the members of the hearing committee asked me, "Why would you ever take your rehabilitated soul and try to practice law?"

We are at a crossroads in this country where we must decide: What will we allow changed people to do? If we believe in second chances, then at some point we have to get out of the way and let them go as far as they can go. This benefits us all. I used to think I could out-work, out-maneuver, out-network, and out-hustle the second prison, but it eventually catches up with you. It's always there, waiting to tell you "no."

Today, I am a productive member of society. I'm putting my law training into use in my role at Prison Fellowship, but am still denied the opportunity to actually practice law. I'm living proof that those in prison can be rehabilitated, but also that opportunities are often denied to us despite that change. There is still work to do to bring about justice that restores.

By now, we hope you better understand the challenges facing the American criminal justice system, and why it is essential that Christians come alongside prisoners and their families, advocate for reform, minister to victims of crime, and unlock the second prison that affects so many people.

You've heard the outrageous statistics: 2.2 million people are behind bars, 1 in 28 children has a mother or father in prison, and approximately 1 in 3 Americans has a criminal record. More than 29,000 people on average will be arrested each day this year.

Something is dangerously out of balance in the American criminal justice system. Crime and incarceration are complex problems, and the system is broken in many ways. But we believe there is hope, because there are simple things that ordinary people can do to bring restoration and redemption to the system.

These numbers, which represent real people, are not an insurmountable hurdle, but an invitation and an opportunity. Jesus said, "Truly I tell you, whatever you did for one of the least of these brothers and sisters of mine, you did for me" (see Matthew 25:40). This book is not only about evaluating how we think about crime and incarceration in light of our faith, but about taking action inspired by that evaluation. As James 2:17 reminds us, "Faith by itself, if it is not accompanied by action, is dead."

You've read real-life stories in this book. Now it's time to notice people in your congregation and community impacted by crime and incarceration, hear their stories, pray for them, and serve them.

In this final chapter, we want to help you move from awareness to action by showing you how people and churches across the country have applied the Bible's calling to both remember those in prison and seek justice. As Christ walked and lived among us, so we are called to minister to people whose lives have been broken by crime and incarceration in up-close and personal ways. We can't let the complexity and immensity of the problem keep us from getting started. At prisonfellowship. org/outrageousjustice, you will find links and resources to all the action steps we discuss. There are many opportunities, both big and small, to help you get started.

From awareness to action: opportunities to respond

So, where to begin? It starts with awareness. If you haven't already, we suggest that you gather with fellow believers to complete the *Outrageous Justice* small-group study (you can find more information at prisonfellowship.org/outrageousjustice). Learn as much as you can about the criminal justice system. Listen to the stories of formerly incarcerated people, victims, and families. Then, act on what you've learned.

As you talk together about these issues, think carefully about the words you are using to refer to people. It may seem small, but the message we send with our language can make a world of difference, and over time, it can fuel changes in cultural perceptions. Practice talking about people as individuals made in the image of God. Use their circumstance as a descriptor rather than a noun ("people with a criminal history" instead of "felons" or "ex-offenders," and "men and women in prison" instead of "inmates"). Some people who have been victims of crime prefer "survivor" or something that eliminates labels altogether like "person who has been harmed by crime." If you're not sure how to refer to their experience, just ask! Practice this within your small group.

You can also connect with Prison Fellowship on social media to keep apprised of criminal justice reform developments and resources about restoring those impacted by crime and incarceration:

> On Facebook: Like, follow, and get notifications for Prison Fellowship at https://www.facebook.com/PFMinistries

> On Twitter: Follow @JusticeReform and @prisonfellowshp

> On Instagram: Follow @prisonfellowship

> On YouTube: Subscribe to our channel, https://www.youtube.com/user/PrisonFellowshipUSA

Prison Fellowship's vision is to equip Christians to put their faith into action in the public square. When you sign up at prisonfellowship.org/advocacyalerts, you become part of our Justice Advocate network. As a Justice Advocate, you will receive monthly newsletters, get legislative updates, and have the opportunity to take action on justice reform issues. You will have access to digital campaigns that help you identify your elected officials and quickly contact them using model social media posts, emails, and call scripts that we provide. You can help inspire the Church, change the culture, and advance justice that restores.

If you want to take your advocacy a step farther, consider applying to be a Justice Ambassador. Justice Ambassadors are the select Justice Advocates in our network who are equipped by Prison Fellowship to:

- Develop relationships with lawmakers through calls, letters, and in-person meetings to encourage support for justice reforms.

- Write letters to the editor in your local paper reflecting Prison Fellowship's views on justice issues.

- Utilize social media campaigns and online petitions to raise awareness and influence others.

- Host awareness-building events on campus, at church, or in your community.

You can learn more and apply to be a Justice Ambassador at prisonfellowship.org/ambassador.

Dale Kersten of Minnesota is one of our Justice Ambassadors making an impact in advancing justice that restores. "I met with my representative's district director to discuss co-sponsoring the Second Chance Act," says Dale. "The tools I received from Prison Fellowship on making an appointment with a lawmaker and developing a longer-term relationship were very helpful. After a few more meetings, I received word that my representative co-sponsored the legislation. It's exciting to see how effective the Justice Ambassador role can be."

Sammy Perez went from volunteering as a Justice Ambassador to becoming a full-time senior grassroots strategist with Prison Fellowship. "As someone who was formerly incarcerated as a youth, I was grateful for the opportunity to channel my experience and passion as a Justice Ambassador," Sammy says. "I never imagined I would be publishing letters in my local newspaper, sharing my story at events, or talking directly with lawmakers and having them support meaningful justice reforms as a result. And now I'm equipping other Justice Ambassadors to do likewise. It feels incredibly rewarding to know that I'm making a difference for today's youth, so hopefully they won't have to go through what I did."

Justice goes to college

College students are uniquely situated to share and engage their peers in justice reform. You can invite a group of students to go through the *Outrageous Justice* study guide, which will spark discussion about how to apply biblical values in our response to crime and incarceration. Another effective strategy is to set up an event with an existing Christian ministry on campus, where people can listen, learn, and eventually act.

If you're a college student, consider reaching out to partner with student organizations that might be willing co-host a joint event that highlights biblical justice values, features a brief teaching from a pastor or ministry leader, and includes the testimony of someone with a criminal record who can discuss the Church's role and response. This event could also serve as a launch event for small groups to go through the *Outrageous Justice* study guide.

A tabling promotion event is another great way to increase the visibility of the need for justice reform to the broader student body. Set up a table in a high-traffic area of campus with an engagement activity that invites interaction. You could display large portraits of people impacted by crime and incarceration with accompanying quotes, pose questions about the criminal justice system to students and post their responses (followed by the facts) on social media, ask people to sign a criminal justice petition, or invite students to the next event—a film screening.

A film screening can engage a broad audience in a discussion about crime and incarceration. These events include the screening of a movie or documentary with themes of crime and redemption. With the help of Prison Fellowship staff, students create a discussion guide to go along with the film or host a panel of experts to discuss the issues raised in the film.

After holding one or more of these events, you could offer participants the opportunity to put their convictions into action.

You might organize a group to visit elected officials, submit an op-ed on criminal justice to your local or campus newspaper, or visit a youth detention center or nearby jail or prison. You can also organize a legislator "phone slam" by setting up a table in a high-traffic area with the lawmakers' phone numbers and a sample script, so students can flood legislators' phone lines in support of justice reform.

Short-term missions

Another way to advocate for justice that restores is to dedicate one of your church's local mission trips to prison ministry or justice reform activities.

For example, National Community Church (NCC) in Washington, D.C., decided to offer a short-term summer mission trip so that members could learn about justice by serving. Led by David and Kelly Friedlander, a team of about a dozen NCC members flew out to Colorado Springs, where they attended a Prison Fellowship volunteer conference, held a Mother's Day worship service for incarcerated women, and staffed Prison Fellowship's Second Chance 5K in Colorado. The NCC mission team directed the 5K participants along the route and handed out water to runners.

"It was a really moving experience," shares Kelly, who leads Prison Fellowship's marketing, communications, and assessment team. "No one other than me had been in a prison or had prison ministry experience, but they all walked away with a better understanding of the challenges faced by the formerly incarcerated."

Putting a face to the issue

Another avenue for advocacy is through writing and storytelling. Our Justice Ambassadors submit letters to the editor in response to criminal justice issues covered in their local paper. Using the written word to put a face and story to the impact of crime and incarceration is a critical tool to changing hearts and minds. We've trained a variety of people to do that, including former prisoner Keith Brice. "I served 16 months of a 10-year sentence and have experienced firsthand the struggle to secure a job coming out of prison," says Keith. "I decided to become an advocacy writer because I understand what it feels like to be rejected, not because of one's lack of experience, but because of a terrible mistake from my past. I hope my writing shows the real-life impact of incarceration and offers advice and hope to returning citizens."

Jenn Carr, whose story you read earlier, volunteered to share her perspective for this book.

"I saw Prison Fellowship's request for testimonies about how crime and incarceration has impacted you, and I felt compelled to respond," Jenn says. "I was willing to share how my husband was sentenced to 10 plus years in federal prison for wire fraud and the devastating impact it has had on me and my daughters because I believe our experience can help build awareness about disproportional sentencing and lacking prison programs. If more people could see how these policies destroy real families, I believe we could inspire the Church to take action and advance reforms that actually restore our communities."

As you can see, there is no shortage of ways you can advocate to change hearts and minds to advance justice that restores.

Caring for people impacted by crime

Any crime sends ripples through a community, impacting nearly everyone. Obviously, the victim of the crime is directly affected. But others' lives are also disrupted, like the family of the person who is charged with a crime, and the neighbors who worry that their home or neighborhood is not safe. If we care about justice, we need to extend the love of Jesus to everyone who is touched by crime.

As we discussed in Chapter Six, it's likely that someone you know has suffered harm as a victim of crime. We have an opportunity to respond to their physical, emotional, and spiritual needs in the aftermath of crime. It can be as simple as helping to repair a broken door or window after a burglary, or driving someone who has been hurt to the hospital or police station and staying with them as they await treatment or go through reporting. Your church or small group might consider building a relationship with your local sheriff's office, letting them know that you're willing to provide such services for a local person or family affected by a crime. Finally, listening and validating each person's story is critical, and just being there communicates care in a profound way. Having the right words to respond is much less important than being a listening, nonjudgmental presence.

Are you aware of people from your congregation who were recently arrested? Or are currently incarcerated? What about families who have a loved one behind bars? Perhaps you live in a community where this seems to be a common occurrence. Even if you live in a neighborhood that seems untouched by crime, and there don't seem to be individuals or families going through this challenge, statistics indicate otherwise.

If our church community is in a particularly safe or privileged area, it can be easy to think of prison or reentry ministry as a mission project that happens to people "over there." But this appearance can be deceiving. Today, almost every church of every socio-economic background has people affected. Chances are, someone in your congregation has been arrested or entered the criminal justice system at some point. Perhaps they, or even their families, were too ashamed to seek support. Think back to the reaction in your mind when you heard the news. Was it one of disappointment, or perhaps judgment?

For me (Craig), looking back at the road to recovery after my two, very public alcohol-related arrests, there were many believers in my community and church who identified my struggle with addiction—in some cases, before I even identified it—and offered support in a loving manner. One of the police officers involved in my arrest and my Christian attorney encouraged me to seek help through a rehab center. The rehab center where I began to piece my life back together was filled with Christian staff and volunteers who encouraged me and helped me grow spiritually. After rehab, several fellow church members offered to meet with me regularly. They didn't condemn me. They simply modeled Christ and encouraged me forward to sobriety one day at a time.

We hope reading this book will make you more intentional about identifying the people in your congregation, at your job, or in your neighborhood, who are impacted by the criminal justice system in some way. We hope it makes you bolder about meeting their needs and encouraging them. Often it is in those low moments of our lives that unconditional love can speak the loudest. Think of Jesus' response to the woman caught in adultery who was completely scorned by her community and was about to be stoned to death (John 8). Jesus did not excuse her behavior ("go and sin no more"), but He did have compassion for her. He valued her, despite her sin. He recognized that value when everyone else was consumed with condemnation.

In addition to supporting those in your congregation or community during arrest or the criminal justice process, we also encourage you to consider direct ministry to prisoners. As discussed in Chapter Seven, Prison Fellowship offers a range of opportunities to engage those behind bars. If opportunities exist in your area, you may feel called to volunteer with our evangelistic Hope Events, in-prison Bible studies, teaching a class, or serving as role models and life coaches for those in our Academy programs. You can learn more about how to get plugged into volunteer opportunities near you at prisonfellowship.org/action. No matter your location, you can make prisoners and their families a regular topic of prayer.

We can also come alongside the families that prisoners leave behind. Robin Gardner, who told her story in the *Outrageous Justice* study curriculum, said that members of her church would sometimes ask if they could write letters or send books to her husband while he was in prison. She felt she learned who her real friends were because they would ask how she, her children, and her husband were doing. Showing genuine interest in a family's well-being or offering to send a letter to the family member in prison can be a significant gesture for families that may feel excluded or forgotten.

In Chapter Seven, we mentioned Prison Fellowship's Angel Tree program. The simple act of bringing a Christmas gift to a child with a personal message from their incarcerated mom or dad lets them know that their parent loves them and has not forgotten them. Most gifts are delivered by volunteers from local churches at Christmas parties or during visits to families' homes.

One congregation that has embraced ministry to prisoners' families is River Valley Church in Minnesota. In 2014, this extraordinary Angel Tree partner asked if it could serve 1,000 children. We didn't have that many Angel Tree boys and girls left in their immediate area, but, by God's grace, River Valley Church was able to partner with churches in an area with much greater need. For the first time in years, every reachable Angel Tree child in a typically underserved area received a gift in the name of their incarcerated parent.

After witnessing the spiritual influence of Angel Tree at Christmas, many churches feel called to extend their ministry to prisoners' families all year long. If an Angel Tree family is not already involved in a church, the connection provides a great opportunity to invite them to Sunday worship, youth group, or Vacation Bible School. You can learn more about the Angel Tree program at angeltree.org.

Offering opportunities for second chances

As we discussed in the previous chapter, many people find themselves indefinitely stuck in a "second prison" after release. We can "act justly and love mercy" by welcoming those who are returning from prison to our congregations and communities. The transition from prison back to the community is often stressful. While meeting the terms of their probation or parole, people struggle to access housing, afford food, and find a job, not to mention reengage in relationships with their family and friends, often after many years of separation.

Churches across the country have partnered with Prison

Fellowship to provide resources and support for men and women returning from prison. For example, the aptly named Hope Community in Detroit holds reentry network meetings. Every second Saturday morning of the month, volunteers meet with returning citizens for prayer and devotions, assessment of immediate and long-term needs, and other forms of hands-on support. Participants hear engaging speakers, attend job fairs, and even make trips to the grocery store with volunteers alongside them.

Another church passionate about meeting the needs of the formerly incarcerated is Sonrise Church in Hillsboro, Oregon. Pastor Jerry Metee leads a weekly adults-only service called Light My Way. The service provides formerly incarcerated men with a welcoming place to worship—especially those convicted of sexual offenses, who are unable to attend traditional worship services where children would be present.

Church staff member Angela Cordry helps with the Light My Way ministry and sees firsthand the joy people with a criminal history feel when they're included in a family of believers. "To have a place that treats them with respect and dignity means more to them than anything else," says Cordry. The ministry also has a large volunteer base, whose goal is to simply "show up just to love on these guys," she adds.

And that love goes a long way. The church offers help in many forms, including a food pantry, a clothing closet, and a homeless shelter during winter months. They also created a website that helps with housing searches to assist in finding suitable, affordable places to live within the community.

We encourage you to plan, train, and learn from those who have experience in this work. We also recommend those who mentor and serve returning citizens to do so in groups so there are accountability partners. If you have never experienced incarceration yourself, it can be hard to relate to those returning to society. It's important to include group members and leaders who have been through the criminal justice system themselves and can leverage their own experience as mentors.

While the inner change in someone is the foundation for successful reentry, offering someone with a criminal record a job can not only help them, but can contribute to keeping people from returning to prison. John Schmitt, a senior economist with The Center for Economic and Policy Research, quoted in a San Francisco Chronicle article, says work is a strong deterrent to recidivism. "When people get an opportunity to get a job and make a living, their likelihood of returning to crime goes down dramatically," Schmitt observes. "There is a strong association with people not finding a job and people ending up back behind bars."

If you are a business owner or manager, one step you could take is to hire qualified formerly incarcerated people. While not every situation works out, many people who employ former prisoners find them to be loyal, hard-working employees, grateful to be given a chance after so many doors close in their faces. By giving someone with a record an opportunity to prove themselves, you can help them provide for themselves and their families.

For example, Arthur Medina was sent to prison as a very young man to serve 27 years for a murder charge. In prison, he participated in the Prison Fellowship Academy, an intensive, evidence-based program designed to address the roots of his criminal behavior and prepare him for a new life on the outside. When released, he had the opportunity to work for a ventilation company owned by Rick Irvin.

Rick has had many graduates of the Prison Fellowship Academy work for his company. But few of them, he says, are like Arthur Medina.

"When you consider Arthur spent 27 years in prison, 15 of those in solitary confinement, and came out such a polite, respectful young man … well, that's phenomenal," Rick says.

Rick recalls the time one customer called, upset because no one had come out to give him a bid on a job as originally promised. Arthur had not been on the job very long but handled it like a veteran businessman. "The owner of this company is a good Christian man," he calmly told the customer. "And you say you're a man of God. I'm going to get Mr. Irvin to call you back immediately."

The company got the work, a $10,000 job.

Before moving on from the company in 2016, Arthur rose to become vice president of operations and served as a mentor, friend, and Christian witness to other employees.

"Hiring Arthur was the best thing I've done in this company," Rick says.

If you don't own a business, don't dismiss your ability to provide employment assistance. It may be as simple as introducing a friend or business associate. We tend to underestimate the power we have to act as a referral source for someone needing a second chance. We often take for granted how much a strong personal network can contribute to professional success, and that's a resource someone recently home from prison may be lacking. Even assisting someone with writing a résumé can be a huge help.

As part of our efforts to raise awareness about the challenges people with a criminal record face, Prison Fellowship established April as Second Chance Month in 2017. Celebrating Second Chance Month includes hosting Second Chance prayer walks and 5K events, "Second Chance Sunday" services at churches, and coordinated advocacy petitions and social media campaigns. In 2018, we successfully lobbied the Administration and Congress to issue a presidential proclamation and pass a Senate resolution declaring April Second Chance Month. Over a dozen states and localities did likewise. The Second Chance Month initiative has grown to include more than 250 partner organizations, congregations and businesses. In 2017, Second Chance Month coverage reached an estimated 146 million followers on social media, and that increased to over 800 million in 2018. Given the tremendous response in just a few years, we look forward to building on this effort every April for years to come. We hope you'll join us. You can learn more at prisonfellowship.org/secondchances.

Since Prison Fellowship's founding in 1976, we have sought to restore all those affected by crime and incarceration by fostering a growing Christian community inside America's prisons. We also work to prepare welcoming churches and communities on the outside for those who return home. Along the way, we bear witness to miracles of transformation as the Gospel takes root in dark places through the faithfulness of thousands of volunteers, intercessors, and financial partners.

However, all those efforts are undermined if the underlying criminal justice system is plagued by unfair sentencing, a corrosive prison culture, neglect of victims, and other ills that run counter to God's outrageous justice. The good news is that persistent, values-based advocacy can change the system for the better. We know because it already has.

Since the 1980s, when Prison Fellowship began concerted criminal justice reform efforts, advocates like you have helped to ensure prisoners' religious liberty. Advocates have helped protect men and women from the scourge of prison rape. Advocates have helped Prison Fellowship reduce the prison time that people will serve by more than a million years collectively while reducing crime in the communities to which they return.

In 2017, Prison Fellowship collaborated with prominent Christian leaders and organizations to launch the Justice Declaration. The Justice Declaration is a unified call to create a justice system that is fair and redemptive for all. It exhorts the Church to exercise its unique mandate and unparalleled capacity to confront the staggering crisis of crime and incarceration in America and to respond with restorative solutions for communities, victims, and individuals responsible for crime. (To add your name, visit prisonfellowship.org/justice-declaration.)

Much more remains to be done, and your voice is needed now more than ever. Join us as we continue to visit the prisoner and advocate for those affected by crime and incarceration. Together we can experience an amazing awakening to the depths of God's grace, mercy, and justice.

About the Authors

This book was created by a team of criminal justice experts at Prison Fellowship, in partnership with A Powerful Story writing services.

Craig DeRoche is president of the Twelves, a faith-based addiction recovery organization. He formerly served in leadership at Prison Fellowship and as the Michigan Speaker of the House.

Heather Rice-Minus is senior vice president of advocacy & church mobilization for Prison Fellowship. She holds a law degree from George Mason University School of Law.

Jesse Wiese is national director for Academy advancement for Prison Fellowship. He holds a law degree from Regent University School of Law.

Prison Fellowship is the nation's largest Christian nonpro it serving prisoners, former prisoners, and their families, and a leading advocate for criminal justice reform. Established on the belief that all people are created in God's image and that no life is beyond His reach, Prison Fellowship takes a restorative approach to all those affected by crime and incarceration. Prison Fellowship was founded in 1976 by Charles Colson, a former aide to President Nixon who served seven months in federal prison for a Watergate-related crime. Today we strive to make prisons safer and more rehabilitative, advance criminal justice reforms, and support prisoners, their families, and their communities.

A Powerful Story writing services comes alongside businesses, nonpro its, and individuals to help them tell their story in a clear and compelling way. They provide creative direction, project management, collaborative writing, and editing. Learn more at www.apowerfulstory.com.

Acknowledgements

This book could not have been written without the support and leadership of Prison Fellowship's board of directors and its president and chief executive officer, James J. Ackerman. Alyson R. Quinn greatly improved this book in her role as our staff editor. Other Prison Fellowship employees contributed to making this book a great resource, including: Sam Dye, Kelly Friedlander, Doris Girgis, Topher Hall, Dan Kingery, Sara Marlin, Will Riddle, Liz Stanosheck, and Kate Trammell.

NOTES

Chapter One: Outrageous Justice

1   Mariel Alper, et al., *2018 Update on Prisoner Recidivism: A 9-Year Follow-Up Period (2005-2014)*, Bureau of Justice Statistics (May 2018), https://www.bjs.gov/content/pub/pdf/18upr9yfup0514.pdf.

2   Danielle Kaeble & Mary Cowhig, *Correctional Population in the United States, 2016*, Bureau of Justice Statistics, April 2018, https://www.bjs.gov/content/pub/pdf/cpus16.pdf.

3   E. Ann Carson, *Prisoners in 2016*, Bureau of Justice Statistics, January 2018, https://www.bjs.gov/content/pub/pdf/p16.pdf.

4   John Gramlich, *America's Incarceration Rate is at a Two-Decade Low*, Pew Research Center (May 2018), http://www.pewresearch.org/fact-tank/2018/05/02/americas-incarceration-rate-is-at-a-two-decade-low/.

5   Kaeble, *supra* note 2 at 1.

6   Kaeble, *supra* note 2 at 1.

7   The Pew Charitable Trusts, *Collateral Costs: Incarceration's Effect on Economic Mobility*, The Pew Charitable Trusts (2010), http://www.pewtrusts.org/~/media/legacy/uploadedfiles/pcs_assets/2010/collateralcosts1pdf.pdf.

8   Carson, *supra* note 3, at 8.

9   Charles Colson, Justice That Restores, at 10 (Cahners Business Information, Inc. 2000).

Chapter Two: Justice That Respects: What Is "Just Process" and Why Does It Matter?

10 Nick Pinto, *The Bail Trap*, N.Y. Times Magazine, Aug. 13, 2015, http://www.nytimes.com/2015/08/16/magazine/the-bail-trap.html?_r=0

11 Zhen Zeng, *Jail Inmates in 2016*, Bureau of Justice Statistics (February 2018), https://www.bjs.gov/content/pub/pdf/ji16.pdf.

12 Teresa Wiltz, *Locked Up: Is Cash Bail on the Way Out*, Pew Charitable Trust, March 2017, http://www.pewtrusts.org/en/research-and-analysis/blogs/stateline/2017/03/01/locked-up-is-cash-bail-on-the-way-out.

13 The Code of Hammurabi (L.W. King trans., Lillian Goldman Law Library, (2008), available at http://avalon.law.yale.edu/ancient/hamframe.asp.

14 Dan Jones, *The Mad King and Magna Carta*, Smithsonian Magazine, July 2015, http://www.smithsonianmag.com/history/mad-king-magna-carta-180955745/?no-ist.

15 Sir William Blackstone, Commentaries on the Laws of England, (Oxford: Printed at the Clarendon Press, 1765-1769), available at http://avalon.law.yale.edu/subject_menus/blackstone.asp.

16 Blackstone, *supra* note 15 at Book I, 129, 134, 138.

17 The Declaration of Independence para. 2 (U.S. 1776), available at http://www.archives.gov/exhibits/charters/declaration_transcript.html.

18 Harry R. Dammer, *Religion in Corrections*, in The Encyclopedia of Crime and

PUNISHMENT 1375, (Wesley G. Jennings, et al. eds., 2002), available at http://www.
scranton.edu/faculty/dammerh2/ency-religion.shtml.

19 Dammer, *supra* note 18.

20 Dammer, *supra* note 18.

21 Lauren Sullivan, *Timeline: Solitary Confinement in U.S. Prisons*, National Public Radio
    (July 26, 2006), http://www.npr.org/templates/story/story.php?storyId=5579901.

22 Dammer, *supra* note 18.

23 Wayne Jackson, *The Theological Implications of the Trial of Jesus- Part 2*,
    ChristianCourier.com (July 26, 2006), https://www.christiancourier.com/articles/705-
    theological-implications-of-the-trial-of-jesus-part-2.

24 *Foster v. Chatman*, 136 S. Ct. 1737 (2016).

25 *Foster*, 136 S. Ct. at 1737-1738.

26 *Foster*, 136 S. Ct. at 1758.

27 Radley Balko, *The Untouchables: America's Misbehaving Prosecutors, And
    The System That Protects Them*, The Huffington Post (Aug. 1, 2013), http://
    www.huffingtonpost.com/2013/08/01/prosecutorial-misconduct-new-orleans-
    louisiana_n_3529891.html.

28 United States Sentencing Commission, 2017 Sourcebook of Federal Sentencing
    Statistics, United States Sentencing Commission (2018), https://www.ussc.
    gov/sites/default/files/pdf/research-and-publications/annual-reports-and-
    sourcebooks/2017/2017SB_Full.pdf.

29 United States Sentencing Commission, *supra* note 28 at 25.

30 John H. Blume & Rebecca K. Helm, *The Unexonerated: Factually Innocent
    Defendants Who Plead Guilty*, 100 Cornell L. Rev. 157 (2014).

31 Blume, *supra* note 30 at 173-174.

32 *Gideon v Wainwright*, 372 U.S. 335, 343-345 (1963).

33 Maureen McGough, *Indigent Defense: International Perspectives and Research
    Needs*, National Institute of Justice (October 2011), https://www.ncjrs.gov/pdffiles1/
    nij/235895.pdf.

34 The National Registry of Exonerations, *Exonerations in 2017*, The National Registry of
    Exonerations (March 2018), http://www.law.umich.edu/special/exoneration/Documents/
    ExonerationsIn2017.pdf.

35 The National Registry of Exonerations, *supra* note 34.

36 The National Registry of Exonerations, *Browse Cases: Detailed View,* The National
    Registry of Exonerations, http://www.law.umich.edu/special/exoneration/Pages/
    detaillist.aspx. (filtered to 2017 cases only).

37 The National Registry of Exonerations, *supra* note 36 (filtered for 2017 cases with
    false confessions only).

38 The National Registry of Exonerations, *supra* note 36 (filtered for 2017 cases with
    official misconduct only).

39 The National Registry of Exonerations, *supra* note 36 (filtered for 2017 cases with an
    exoneration occurring because of DNA evidence or mistaken witness identification only).

Chapter Three: Justice That Harms: How Did We Get Off Track?

40   Gary Fields & John R. Emshwiller, *A Sewage Blunder Earns Engineer a Criminal Record*, The Wall Street Journal (Dec. 12, 2011), http://online.wsj.com/article_email/SB10001424052970204903804577082770135339442-lMyQjAxMTAxMDEwMjExNDIyWj.html.

41   Kaeble, *supra* note 2 at 1.

42   Gramlich, *supra* note 4.

43   Federal Bureau of Investigation, *Crime in the United States by Volume and Rate per 100,000 Inhabitants, 1996–2015*, U.S. Department of Justice (2016), https://ucr.fbi.gov/crime-in-the-u.s/2015/crime-in-the-u.s.-2015/tables/table-1; Federal Bureau of Investigation, *Crime in the United States by Volume and Rate per 100,000 Inhabitants, 1995–2014*, U.S. Department of Justice (2015), https://ucr.fbi.gov/crime-in-the-u.s/2014/crime-in-the-u.s.-2014/tables/table-1; Federal Bureau of Investigation, *Crime in the United States by Volume and Rate per 100,000 inhabitants, 1997–2016*, U.S. Department of Justice (2017), https://ucr.fbi.gov/crime-in-the-u.s/2016/crime-in-the-u.s.-2016/topic-pages/tables/table-1.

44   Adam Gelb & Jacob Denney, *National Prison Rate Continues to Decline Amid Sentencing, Re-Entry Reforms*, Pew Charitable Trust (January 2018), http://www.pewtrusts.org/en/research-and-analysis/articles/2018/01/16/national-prison-rate-continues-to-decline-amid-sentencing-re-entry-reforms.

45   United States Sentencing Commission, *supra* note 28 at 25.

46   Federal Bureau of Investigation, *Table 18: Estimated Number of Arrests – United States*, 2016, Department of Justice (2017), https://ucr.fbi.gov/crime-in-the-u.s/2016/crime-in-the-u.s.-2016/tables/table-18.

47   Kaeble, *supra* note 2 at 4.

48   Kaeble, *supra* note 2 at 2.

49   Kaeble, *supra* note 2 at 2.

50   The National Registry of Exonerations, *supra* note 34.

51   Annie E. Casey, *A Shared Sentence*, The Annie E. Casey Foundation (April 2016), http://www.aecf.org/m/resourcedoc/aecf-asharedsentence-2016.pdf.

52   Timothy Hughes & Doris James Wilson, *Reentry Trends in the U.S.*, Bureau of Justice Statistics (May 2018), https://www.bjs.gov/content/reentry/reentry.cfm.

53   Carson, *supra* note 3 at 11.

54   Anastasia Christman & Michelle Natividad Rodriguez, *Research Supports Fair Chance Policies*, The National Employment Law Project (August 2016), https://www.nelp.org/publication/research-supports-fair-chance-policies/#_edn1.

55   Carson, *supra* note 3 at 13.

56   Policy and Program Studies Service, *State and Local Expenditures on Corrections and Education*, U.S. Department of Education (July 2016), https://www2.ed.gov/rschstat/eval/other/expenditures-corrections-education/brief.pdf.

57   Bureau of Prisons, *FY 2019 Budget Request At A Glance*, Department of Justice (2018), https://www.justice.gov/jmd/page/file/1033161/download; Federal Bureau of Prisons, *Statistics, Federal Bureau of Prisons* (February 2019), https://www.bop.gov/about/statistics/population_statistics.jsp.

58 Spending on each individual held in federal prisons is $39,000 based on a budget of $7.1 billion and a population of 184,000.

59 Carson, *supra* note 3 at 1; Bureau of Justice Statistics, *Prisoners 1925-81*, U.S. Department of Justice (December 1982), https://www.bjs.gov/content/pub/pdf/p2581.pdf.

60 Kaeble, *supra* note 2 at 4.

61 Gramlich, *supra* note 4.

62 James J. Stephan, *Census of State and Federal Correctional Facilities, 2005*, Bureau of Justice Statistics (October 2008), https://www.bjs.gov/content/pub/pdf/csfcf05.pdf.

63 Margaret Werner Cahalan, *Historical Corrections Statistics in the United States, 1850 – 1984*, Bureau of Justice Statistics (December 1986), https://www.bjs.gov/content/pub/pdf/hcsus5084.pdf.

64 The Pew Center on the States, *Times Served: The High Cost, Low Return of Longer Prison Terms*, The Pew Center on the States (June 2012), http://www.pewtrusts.org/~/media/legacy/uploadedfiles/wwwpewtrustsorg/reports/sentencing_and_corrections/prisontimeservedpdf.pdf.

65 Jeremy Travis, et al., THE GROWTH OF INCARCERATION IN THE UNITED STATES: EXPLORING CAUSES AND CONSEQUENCES 70 (Nat'l Academies Press 2014).

66 Eric E. Sterling, *Drug Laws and Snitching: A Primer*, WGBH Educational Foundation (2014), http://www.pbs.org/wgbh/pages/frontline/shows/snitch/primer/.

67 Paula M. Ditton & Doris James Wilson, *Truth in Sentencing in State Prisons*, Bureau of Justice Statistics (January 1999), https://bjs.gov/content/pub/pdf/tssp.pdf.

68 Travis, *supra* note 65 at 83.

69 Harvey Silvergate, THREE FELONIES A DAY: HOW THE FEDS TARGET THE INNOCENT (Encounter Books June 2011).

70 Kathleen F. Brickley, *Criminal Mischief: The Federalization of American Criminal Law*, 46 Hastings L. J. 1135, 1139 (1995).

71 John S. Baker, *Revisiting the Explosive Growth of Federal Crimes*, Heritage Foundation (June 16, 2008), http://www.heritage.org/research/reports/2008/06/revisiting-the-explosive-growth-of-federal-crimes.

72 Baker, *supra* note 71 at 1.

73 John C. Coffee, Jr., *Does "Unlawful" Mean "Criminal"?: Reflections on the Disappearing Tort/Crime Distinction in American Law*, 71 B.U. L. Rev. 193, 216 (1991) (stating "there are over 300,000 federal regulations that may be enforced criminally.").

74 Coffee, *supra* note 73 at 216; *See also* Susan R. Klein & Ingrid B. Grobey, *Debunking Claims of Over-Federalization of Criminal Law*, 62 Emory L.J. 1, 28 (2012) ("An enormous number of new regulatory crimes were enacted in the period 1980-2011, so many that we were unable to count even a fraction of them.").

75 OJJDP, *Juveniles in Court: Delinquency Cases*, Office of Juvenile Justice and Delinquency Prevention (March 2018), https://www.ojjdp.gov/ojstatbb/court/qa06204.asp?qaDate=2015.

76 *United States v. McNab*, 324 F.3d 1266 (11ᵗʰ Cir. 2003); *Reining in Overcriminalization: Assessing the Problems, Proposing Solutions: Hearing Before the Subcomm. on Crime, Terrorism, and Homeland Sec. of the H. Comm. on the Judiciary*, 111th Cong. 2 (2010)

(statement of Robert "Bobby" Unser), *available at* http://judiciary.house.gov/_files/ hearings/printers/111th/111-151_58476.pdf; Gary Fields & John R. Emshwiller, *As Criminal Laws Proliferate, More Are Ensnared*, The Wall Street Journal (July 23, 2011), http://online.wsj.com/article/SB10001424052748703749504576172714184601654.html.

77 These solutions were developed by The Heritage Foundation. *See* Brian W. Walsh, *The Criminal Intent Report: Congress Is Eroding the Mens Rea Requirement in Federal Criminal Law*, Heritage Foundation (May 14, 2010), http://thf_media. s3.amazonaws.com/2010/pdf/wm_2900.pdf

78 The Pew Charitable Trusts, *supra* note 7 at 18.

79 The Pew Charitable Trusts, *supra* note 7 at 18.

80 The Pew Charitable Trusts, *supra* note 7 at 19.

81 The Pew Charitable Trusts, *supra* note 7 at 18.

82 Carson, *supra* note 3 at 13.

Chapter Four: Justice That Restores: Why Do We Punish Crime?

83 Kaeble, *supra* note 2 at 4.

84 Lorana Bartels, *Swift and certain sanctions: Is it time for Australia to bring some HOPE into the criminal justice system?*, 39 Crim. L.J. 53 (2015).

85 Beau Kilmer, et al., *Efficacy of Frequent Monitoring with Swift, Certain, and Modest Sanctions for Violations: Insights from South Dakota's 24/7 Sobriety Project* 103 Am. J. Public Health 37 (January 2013).

86 C. S. Lewis, *The Humanitarian Theory of Punishment*, 13 Issues in Religion Psychotherapy 147 (April 1987).

87 Hughes, *supra* note 52.

88 Chris Marshall, *Divine Justice as Restorative Justice*, Center for Christian Ethics 19 (2012), https://www.baylor.edu/content/services/document.php/163072.pdf.

Chapter Five: Justice That Fits: What Is Proportional Punishment?

89 Joel Goh, *Proportionality - An Unattainable Ideal in the Criminal Justice System*, 2 Manchester Student L. Rev. 41 (2013).

90 *Solem v. Helm*, 463 US 277, 288-89 (1983).

91 The National Registry of Exonerations, *supra* note 34.

92 *United States v. Angelos*, 345 F. Supp. 2d 1227 (D. Utah 2004).

93 *Angelos*, 345 F. Supp. 2d at 1230-1232.

94 18 U.S.C.S. §924(c) (2003).

95 *Angelos*, 345 F. Supp. 2d at 1230.

96 *Angelos*, 345 F. Supp. 2d at 1239.

97 *Angelos*, 345 F. Supp. 2d at 1260.

98 *Angelos*, 345 F. Supp. 2d at 1230.

99 *Angelos*, 345 F. Supp. 2d at 1230.

100 *Angelos*, 345 F. Supp. 2d at 1230; *See also Mandatory Minimum Sentencing Laws – The Issues: Before the Subcommittee on Crime, Terrorism and Homeland Security of the H. Comm. on the Judiciary*, 110th Cong. 4 (2007) (Statement of Judge Paul G. Cassell).

101 Greg Jaffe & Sari Horwtiz, *Utah Man whose long drug sentence stirred controversy is released,* Washington Post, June 3, 2016, https://www.washingtonpost.com/politics/president-obama-just-commuted-the-sentences-of-42-people-here-are-their-names/2016/06/03/08f23b7c-29c3-11e6-a3c4-0724e8e24f3f_story.html.

102 Jane Gross, *Born of Grief, 'Three Strikes' Laws Are Being Rethought*, N.Y. Times, Dec. 2, 2013, http://www.nytimes.com/2013/12/02/booming/born-of-grief-three-strikes-laws-are-being-rethought.html?_r=0.

103 Gross, *supra* note 102.

104 Gross, *supra* note 102.

105 Gross, *supra* note 102.

106 Carson, *supra* note 3 at 8.

107 Lynn Langton & Matthew Durose, *Police Behavior during Traffic and Street Stops, 2011*, Bureau of Justice Statistics (September 2013), https://www.bjs.gov/content/pub/pdf/pbtss11.pdf.

108 Langton, *supra* note 107 at 9.

109 Patrick A. Langan, *The Racial Disparity in U.S. Drug Arrests*, Bureau of Justice Statistics (October 1995), http://www.bjs.gov/content/pub/pdf/rdusda.pdf.

110 William Rhodes, et al., *Federal Sentencing Disparity, 2005-2012*, Bureau of Justice Statistics (October 2015), https://www.bjs.gov/content/pub/pdf/fsd0512.pdf.

111 Anti-Drug Abuse Act of 1986, H.R. 5484, 99th Cong. (1986).

112 LaVelle Hendricks, & Angie Wilson, *The Impact of Crack Cocaine on Black America*, 2 Nat'l F. J. Counseling Addiction 1 (2013).

113 Fair Sentencing Act of 2010, S. 1789, 111th Cong. (2010).

114 United States Sentencing Commission, *Report to the Congress: Impact of the Fair Sentencing Act of 2010*, United States Sentencing Commission (August 2015), https://www.ussc.gov/research/congressional-reports/2015-report-congress-impact-fair-sentencing-act-2010.

115 Tex. Penal Code §8.07 (2013); La. Civil Code Art. 29 (1988).

116 Jake Horowitz & Monica Fuhrmann, "States Can Safely Raise Their Felony Theft Thresholds, Research Shows," The Pew Charitable Trust (May 2018), http://www.pewtrusts.org/en/research-and-analysis/articles/2018/05/22/states-can-safely-raise-their-felony-theft-thresholds-research-shows.

117 Prison Fellowship, *The Death Penalty*, Prison Fellowship (2016), http://www.prisonfellowship.org/resources/advocacy/sentencing/the-death-penalty/.

118 Prison Fellowship, *Faith and Justice Fellowship*, Prison Fellowship (2016), https://www.prisonfellowship.org/about/advocacy/landing-pages/faith-and-justice-fellowship/.

Chapter Six: Justice That Listens: What Do Victims Need?

119 Rachel Morgan & Grace Kena, *Criminal Victimization, 2016*, Bureau of Justice Statistics (December 2017), https://www.bjs.gov/content/pub/pdf/cv16.pdf.

120 Morgan, *supra* note 119 at 1.

121 Morgan, *supra* note 119 at 5.

122 Erika Harrell, *Victims of Identity Theft, 2014*, Bureau of Justice Statistics (September 2015), https://www.bjs.gov/content/pub/pdf/vit14.pdf.

123 Lynn Langton, *Victimizations Not Reported to the Police, 2006-2010*, Bureau of Justice Statistics (August 2012), https://www.bjs.gov/content/pub/pdf/vnrp0610.pdf.

124 Federal Bureau of Investigations, *Crime in the United States 2016: Offenses Cleared*, Federal Bureau of Investigations (2016), https://ucr.fbi.gov/crime-in-the-u.s/2016/crime-in-the-u.s.-2016/topic-pages/clearances.

125 United States Sentencing Commission, *supra* note 28.

126 Del. Code Ann. tit. 11, §9405 (1994); Ga. Code Ann. § 17-17-11 (1995); Neb. Rev. Stat. § 29-120 (2018).

127 Josephine Gittler, *Expanding the Role of Victim in a Criminal Action: An Overview of Issues and Problems*, 11 PEPP. L. REV. 5 (1984).

128 Marlene Young & John Stein, *The History of Crime Victims' Movement in the United States*, Office for Victims of Crime (December 2004), https://www.ncjrs.gov/ovc_archives/ncvrw/2005/pdf/historyofcrime.pdf.

129 Young, *supra* note 128 at 2.

130 Young, *supra* note 128 at 3.

131 Lois Haight Herrington, et al., *Final Report*, President's Task Force on Victims of Crime (December 1982), https://www.ovc.gov/publications/presdntstskforcrprt/87299.pdf.

132 Herrington, *supra* note 131 at 114.

133 Charles Doyle, *Victims' Rights Amendment: A Proposal to Amend the United States Constitution in the 108th Congress*, Congressional Research Service (April 16, 2004), https://royce.house.gov/uploadedfiles/rl31750.pdf.

134 Doyle, *supra* note 133.

135 Crime Victims' Rights Act, 18 U.S.C. § 3771 (2004).

136 Maarten Junst, et al., *Victim Satisfaction with the Criminal Justice System and Emotional Recovery*, 16 Trauma Violence Abuse 336 (2015); Malini Laxminarayan, et al., *Victim Satisfaction with Criminal Justice: A Systematic Review*, 8 Victims Offenders 119 (2013).

137 Young, *supra* note 128 at 2.

138 Douglas N. Evans, *Compensating Victims of Crime*, John Jay College of Criminal Justice (2014), http://www.njjn.org/uploads/digital-library/jf_johnjay3.pdf.

139 Department of Justice, General Administration: Federal Funds, Department of Justice (2018), https://www.whitehouse.gov/sites/whitehouse.gov/files/omb/budget/fy2018/jus.pdf..

140 Evans, *supra* note 138 at 5

141 Evans, *supra* note 138 at 14.

142 Mark Umbrae, *Restorative Justice Through Victim-Offender Mediation: A Multi-site Assessment*, 1 Western Criminology Rev. 1 (1998).

143 Umbrae, *supra* note 142.

144 *See* Colby Itkowitz, *Her son shot their daughters 10 years ago. Then, these Amish families embraced her as a friend.*, The Washington Post (Oct. 1, 2016), https://www.washingtonpost.com/news/inspired-life/wp/2016/10/01/10-years-ago-her-son-killed-amish-children-their-families-immediately-accepted-her-into-their-lives/.

145 Audio: Dylann Roof's Bond Hearing, Released by the Charleston County Governor, available at: http://time.com/time-magazine-charleston-shooting-cover-story/ (last visited Aug. 10, 2016).

146 David Von Drehle, et al., *How Do You Forgive a Murderer?* Time Magazine, Nov. 23, 2015, http://time.com/time-magazine-charleston-shooting-cover-story/.

Chapter Seven: Justice That Transforms: Why Do We Need a Constructive Prison Culture?

147 *CBS* News, *Four female prison guards impregnated by the same inmate*, CBS News (April 24, 2013), http://www.cbsnews.com/news/four-female-prison-guards-impregnated-by-same-inmate/.

148 Governor Larry Hogan, *Governor Larry Hogan Announces Final Detainee Transfer from Baltimore City Detention Center*, Governor Larry Hogan (Aug. 25, 2015), http://governor.maryland.gov/2015/08/25/governor-larry-hogan-announces-final-detainee-transfer-from-baltimore-city-detention-center/.

149 Hughes, *supra* note 52.

150 Alper, *supra* note 1 at 1.

Chapter Eight: Justice That Redeems: How Can We Unlock the "Second Prison"?

151 *Locked Out: Voices From America's Second Prison* (Jesse Wiese ed., 2016).

152 Kaeble, *supra* note 2; The Pew Charitable Trusts, supra note 7; Anastasia Christman & Michelle Natividad Rodriguez, *Research Supports Fair Chance Policies*, The National Employment Law Project (August 2016), https://www.nelp.org/publication/research-supports-fair-chance-policies/#_edn1.

153 Hughes, *supra* note 52.

154 Justice Center, *National Inventory of Collateral Consequences of Conviction*, The Council of State Governments (2018), https://niccc.csgjusticecenter.org/.

155 The Sentencing Project, *Expanding the Vote: Two Decades of Felony Disenfranchisement Reform*, The Sentencing Project (October 2018), https://www.sentencingproject.org/publications/expanding-vote-two-decades-felony-disenfranchisement-reforms/.

156 Prison Fellowship, *10 Most Outrageous Restrictions on People with a Criminal Record*, Prison Fellowship (2017), https://www.prisonfellowship.org/site/wp-content/uploads/2017/04/Top10Outrageous_web.pdf.

157 Prison Fellowship, *supra* note 156.

158 Prison Fellowship, *supra* note 156.

159 Prison Fellowship, *supra* note 156.

160 Prison Fellowship, *supra* note 156.

161 Prison Fellowship, *supra* note 156.

162 Prison Fellowship, *supra* note 156.

163 Cherrie Bucknor & Alan Barber, *The Price We Pay: Economic Costs of Barriers to Employment for Former Prisoners and People Convicted of Felonies*, Center for Economic and Policy Research (June 2016), http://cepr.net/publications/reports/the-price-we-pay-economic-costs-of-barriers-to-employment-for-former-prisoners-and-people-convicted-of-felonies.

164 Jennifer Lundquist, et al., *Does a Criminal Past Predict Worker Performance? Evidence from America's Largest Employer*, Amer. Soc. Rev. (2018), https://academic.oup.com/sf/article-abstract/96/3/1039/4802355?redirectedFrom=fulltext

165 Lundquist, *supra* note 164.

166 Douglas N. Evans, *Punishment Without End*, John Jay College of Criminal Justice (July 2014), https://jjrec.files.wordpress.com/2014/07/jf_johnjay1.pdf.

167 Evans, *supra* note 166 at 1.

168 Alfred Blumstein & Kiminori Nakamura, *Redemption in the Presence of Widespread Criminal Background Checks*, 47 Criminology 327 (May 2009).

169 Blumstein, *supra* note 168 at 338-340.

170 Blumstein, *supra* note 168 at 344.

171 Blumstein, *supra* note 168 at 338-340.

Chapter Nine: Justice That Responds: A Call to Act Justly and Love Mercy

172 Kaeble, supra note 152.

173 Federal Bureau of Investigation, *supra* note 43.

174 Wendy Lee, *Felons Barred from Constructing Apple's Campus,* SF GATE, (Apr. 4, 2015), http://www.sfgate.com/business/article/Felons-barred-from-constructing-Apple-s-campus-6178429.php.